Added Value

The alchemy of brand-led growth

Added Value

The alchemy of brand-led growth

Mark Sherrington

First published 2003 by
PALGRAVE MACMILLAN
Houndmills, Basingstoke, Hampshire RG21 6XS and
175 Fifth Avenue, New York, N.Y. 10010
Companies and representatives throughout the world

PALGRAVE MACMILLAN is the global academic imprint of the Palgrave Macmillan division of St. Martin's Press, LLC and of Palgrave Macmillan Ltd. Macmillan® is a registered trademark in the United States, United Kingdom and other countries. Palgrave is a registered trademark in the European Union and other countries.

ISBN 1–4039–0387–5 hardback

This book is printed on paper suitable for recycling and made from fully managed and sustained forest sources.

A catalogue record for this book is available from the British Library.

Library of Congress catalog card No : 2003043143

Editing and origination by
Curran Publishing Services, Norwich

10 9 8 7 6 5 4 3 2
12 11 10 09 08 07 06 05 04 03

Printed and bound in Great Britain by
Creative Print & Design (Wales), Ebbw Vale

To Sherry and Jessica Robyn, two people who never got to see the difference they made to my life.

CONTENTS

LIST OF FIGURES

ACKNOWLEDGEMENTS

As is often the way, the author got a lot of help. Everyone in Added Value and its clients over the years contributed to the thinking, the tools and the examples. My thanks to all of you but especially Peter (times two), Paul (times two), Janine, Charles, David (times two), Andy and Malcolm. In terms of the development of the material and the production, Emma Douglas and Nighat Bandey were my rock. Dave Evans added thick layers of polish to the writing and editing: I am eternally in his debt.

Alan McWalter, James Hill, Keith Weed, Martin Glenn, Nick Fell and my dear friend and mentor, Andrew Seth were my inspiration for the 'stuff that gets in the way' of making good marketing work in business. They should know having got round the 'stuff' to deliver great marketing in their respective businesses.

My wife was no help at all – she obstinately refused to read any of the drafts claiming to have better things to do – but she was very understanding and is inspirational and gorgeous in every other way.

Sir Martin Sorrell and Graham Mackay, CEOs of WPP and SABMiller respectively, made it possible to get the time to write the book and to move back into a marketing director's job to be hoisted by my own petard.

My grateful thanks to all of you.

COPYRIGHT ACKNOWLEDGEMENTS

Figures 1.1, 2.1, 3.1 and 4.1 are published with the permission of Getty Images.

Appendix 1 is copyright Michael Harvey and Malcolm Evans, and was first published in the *International Journal of Market Research*, April 2001.

Appendix 2 is copyright Paul McGowan and Flemming from Thygesen, and was first published in the *International Journal of Market Research*, April 2002.

I also gratefully acknowledge permission from Added Value to reproduce a number of charts on which they hold the copyright.

Mark Sherrington

Can I start by saying...

Business only goes in two directions: up and down. The bottom line is: if you aren't growing, you're dying. Of course, in theory you could stagnate, but any ex-CEO will tell you that marking time – or even biding it – is simply a euphemism for going down the pan. Companies are addicted to growth – and, like the worst addict, they will do whatever it takes to get it. They can buy, they can cut, they can rob, they can steal – but time has shown that marketing is the surest fix of all.

We all recognise 'marketing' when it drops onto our desks: focus group reports, consumer surveys, market segmentation strategies, that kind of thing. But how all this turns into stronger, more profitable brands is often a little obscure. Research and analysis are a big part of good marketing, but even truly great analysis pulls up some way short of great marketing. Great analysis might be a necessary cause for that great creative idea, but that doesn't mean it's a sufficient one. And even if you have come up with that great idea, all the research and analysis in the world are no guarantee that it will translate into great growth and profits. And that, at the end of the day, is what marketing is all about.

Truly great marketing is a rare and precious thing – and who would deny it's worth its weight in gold? It's certainly the kind of gold that stacks up in ingots in the vault; just ask Coca-Cola, Nike or Unilever. But great marketing is more than that. It's also the kind of gold with the power to make you stop and gawp, as if you'd stubbed your toe on a Krugerrand on the beach. Remember the first time you walked into Nike World? Or the first time you picked up a tub of Ben and Jerry's? Or when you first went into Pret A Manger and realised that everything before had been just another sandwich shop? It's so obvious when great marketing really works that it can look simple; but producing that great marketing is one of the most fiendishly elusive tasks in business.

So what turns great research and great analysis into great marketing? What's the difference between 'Oh, I get it' and 'I've got to get it!'? The answer is something that could be called 'insight alchemy'.

Until Harry Potter saved the day, alchemy used to get a bad press. Most people saw it as the hobby of choice for misguided medieval anoraks. But for hundreds of years, alchemy engaged some of the brightest minds of Europe. Even Sir Isaac Newton took time out from dodging apples to devote a considerable amount of his career to alchemical researches. The alchemists were seekers after gold. They believed there was a way to produce gold from other metals such as mercury, copper and lead – and they were deadly serious about it. Much as market researchers do today, they pored over arcane texts and sought meaning in occult symbols and obscure data. They squandered vast sums of their patrons' money on state-of-the-art lab equipment and lavish experiments to test their theories. But however well prepared they were and however well funded, all alchemists needed a special substance to create the gold they desired – something they called 'the Philosopher's Stone'. Over the centuries, many alchemists claimed to have produced it (although it defies the laws of modern chemistry) and some did indeed become mysteriously – and seriously – rich.

As with alchemy, so with marketing. All good marketers are seekers of a kind of Philosopher's Stone – some kind of inspiration, a certain magic – that turns great research and analysis into marketing gold. I've closely observed the alchemical processes of marketing in action throughout my career – first at my alma mater, Unilever, and then at the international marketing consultancy, Added Value, which I set up with colleagues more than 14 years ago. During this time I've been lucky enough to work with many fine businesses, and scores of world class brands. From this experience and with the help of many colleagues and clients (yes, it's true, consultants and agencies probably learn as much from their clients as they give them in return), I and the team at Added Value distilled a process for creating growth in brands and business.

We call this process 'the Five 'I's' and it is infallible – or at least it would be, if it weren't for all the stuff that gets in the way. And believe me, it's not just the competition that gets in the way. My own experience of working in large companies (and I have found this is true is for any large business) is that it's like trying to score a goal in soccer, but first having to get the ball past 10 of your own players.

The Five 'I's process we developed at Added Value provides the structure for this book, with a separate chapter on each 'I':

- Insight
- Ideas
- Innovation
- Impact
- Investment return

Every chapter contains practical tools and approaches for tackling each of these steps, set out in simple terms, with clear examples. And at the end of each of these chapters, there's a short section discussing the stuff that gets in the way – the reasons businesses might find each of these processes difficult.

Much of the material you'll find here is based on tools developed at Added Value and real examples drawn from the work of the consultancy. There are also illustrations and stories that I've picked up secondhand over the years – and I apologise in advance if I haven't been able to acknowledge all my sources. My friends in the profession will also spot the fruits of our many long and passionate discussions, for which I am very grateful. But much in this book is personal: the polemic, the mistakes and the jokes. And I'm sorry, but I make no apologies for any of them.

Good comedians tell jokes in the first person. The humour of the joke is not improved by some complicated explanation of the relationship of the teller to the protagonist. Nor is it made funnier by empirical research to prove its credibility. A joke about mothers-in-law isn't made funnier by saying, 'You'll like this joke, it was told by three of the funniest comedians in the USA.' And you won't improve it by explaining how research proves that the point of the joke is true for the majority of mothers-in-law. The audience just want to hear the joke, and they will laugh if they recognise some comic or ironic truth in it.

I hope you'll recognise some truths in this book. The penny dropping, the word on the tip of the tongue, the thing you wished you'd said ... these are some of the Philosopher's Stones that insight alchemy seeks. And the Five 'I's is a process that can take you to within touching distance of that marketing gold. But at best, it's the baton delivered at the final leg of the 4 x 100, it's the perfectly weighted pass into the box, the iron out of the rough onto the green... the problem is, the finish is up to you.

And that, I'm afraid, is the problem with all business books: a great business book does not necessarily make a great business. The irony of Michael Porter's books on competitive advantage, generally regarded as great business books, is that being available to all, both you and your competitors, they offer no competitive advantage at all. But, come to that, a great Tiger Woods book is not enough to make you a great golfer. In any field, understanding is one thing, but the application is something very different.

The true insight alchemist is the person who can bridge that gap.

The Five 'I's

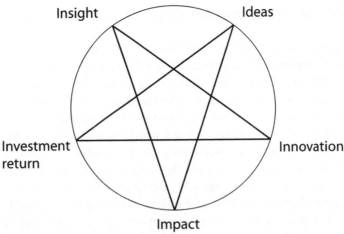

Figure I.1 The Five 'I's

Appearances can be deceptive. Companies like to boast of their unity of purpose, their mission, their strategic vision; but too many organisations work without any real plot, and if they do have one, it's often much too easy to lose it. How many times do you find that the finance people are speaking Cantonese, while the marketers all speak Mandarin? It may look like they're using the same language, but very little real communication is occurring. How often do the most innovative companies fail because their innovations occur in a strategic vacuum, or because they require new skills that the business has no hope of obtaining? And how many companies employ the most wildly creative types but fail to use their insights simply because there is no mechanism to make that happen? Instead, their best ideas are stacked up like Cold War missiles in a silo and never get the chance to fire.

The Five 'I's process provides an antidote to this kind of common corporate malaise. That's because it's all about knitting a business together, allowing a company to act on its insights and to develop its innovations effectively. The Five 'I's also help all parts of a company to speak the same language and to aim at the same simple target: growth.

So how do businesses grow? Assuming we are talking about growth in profits (and shareholders will be quick to point out that we should be!), there are only three ways:

- A business can make **acquisitions**.
- It can **cut costs**.
- It can **increase revenues** (so called top-line growth).

Good businesses will try to grow in all three ways, and marketing has an important part to play in each of them – although you might not think so at first.

Certainly, the role of marketing in the process of acquisition may not immediately be apparent. This, after all, is the domain of the finance wonks, right? Wrong. When the accountants tot up the figures, they find that most businesses have valuations far above the value of their tangible assets. In fact, around two-thirds of the value of most stock markets is based on intangible value. This could reflect goodwill or know-how, but mostly it's based on reputation which, in turn, is based firmly on marketing. It's perhaps surprising, then, that so few businesses apply the same rigour to appraising reputation or brand value, as they do to appraising the financials. They should. As we'll see in the later chapter on investment return, marketing's real contribution to the acquisition process is to set out the top-line growth potential of the target. When Campbell's acquired Danone's soup business in France in 1996, it did so having completed a five-year marketing plan that, together with the conventional financial analysis, gave it a much more accurate idea of the real value of that business to its own.

Marketing may not appear to have much to say about cost-cutting either. Certainly, some cynical finance directors believe marketers are the enemies of cost efficiency. And they have a point. By nature, marketers are investors, not cost-cutters, and they are responsible for expenditures, such as research, media and advertising, that are subject to very little scrutiny in comparison with other kinds of capital expenditure. But the Five 'I's process is all about cost efficiency. The basic tools that underpin it are all dedicated to channelling the resources of the business in the most efficient possible way. Good marketers embrace the right kind of cost reduction (and all businesses have costs that can be cut), because it releases money that can be better invested. Of course, the cynical marketer will accuse the finance director of always taking cost savings into short term profits and of being the enemy of long-term brand building investment. That is also quite wrong. Finance directors can be totally responsive to a business case that demonstrates attractive returns, and shareholders regularly invest in companies with profits that are low in the short term but high in the long term.

The problem is simply that many marketers are very poor at making the case, financial and business, for marketing.

So marketing has an important part to play in growth through both acquisitions and cost-cutting. But its most important role is reserved for the most important source of growth – the creation of top-line, demand-led growth. After all, there are only so many businesses that can be acquired, and there is a limit to the costs that can be reduced, but top-line growth will take you as far as your enthusiasm, ingenuity and creativity will allow.

Unfortunately, many definitions of marketing fail to capture this idea, focusing instead on the notion of marketing as a process:

Marketing is the management process responsible for identifying, anticipating and satisfying customer requirements profitably.

Fair enough, perhaps, but hardly inspiring. The best definition of marketing is one that makes it clear that the difference between marketing strategy and business strategy is merely one of emphasis. This definition, for example, brings out the true purpose of marketing:

Marketing is about creating top-line growth, inspiring the organisation to persuade people to buy more and pay more.

If top-line growth is the purpose of marketing, then the Five 'I's is the process that sets out how this can be best achieved.
The Five 'I's is depicted as a circle because it is an ongoing, cyclical process in which each element is mutually supportive. Here it is, expressed as a series of questions:

1. **Insight.** What is your insight? It can come from anywhere: other people, the market, technology, the competition, trends or the value chain, but beware of consumers! As we'll see, they are perhaps the most over-rated of all sources of insight.
2. **Ideas.** What strategy, or big idea, for the business and the brand does your insight inspire?
3. **Innovation.** What will you change as a result of this idea? What is the innovation?
4. **Impact.** How will you make the best impact for the right money?
5. **Investment return.** How will you know this is working? Can you be sure you're maximising your return on marketing investment (ROMI)? What are the key performance indicators (KPIs) that you can use to check and adjust your marketing?

Insight is at the heart of the process, and it may be the most logical place to start, but don't forget that the Five 'I's is a loop that can be super-charged from any starting point. You can cut in at any stage with an intervention that might challenge the thinking behind the process or even create new sources for growth. For example, in most companies there is an annual review as part of the planning process where, in effect, the KPIs of the business or brand are appraised. This is very often the moment when either the KPIs themselves are challenged (that's when you discover you're measuring the wrong things) or the results throw out insights that cause a change in strategy and implementation.

In one such review, the then brand manager of Guinness in Ireland reported that Guinness had had a good year because it had grown its share of stout (i.e. black beers like Guinness), a category that the brand already dominated. However, the statement concealed a darker truth, because the stout category overall had declined and in fact, sales of Guinness were down. The marketing director pointed out that this had actually been a very bad year. The clue was right there in the words, 'sales of Guinness were down'. What followed was a total overhaul of the brand. Data showing that it had lost its relevance to younger Irish drinkers led to a refocus on youth which, in turn, produced innovation in the form of Extra Cold Guinness. The result was that the brand soon returned to growth.

Similarly, intervention often comes at the Impact stage of the process. The agency struggles to respond to the brief, the brief is challenged, fresh insight is gathered and the process moves forward with more pace and purpose. I saw this in the mid-1980s, when I was working on a campaign for the old Persil washing powder. At the time, this was being steadily displaced by Persil Automatic and so only merited a fairly low budget poster campaign. But posters focus the mind more than any other medium. In writing the brief for the poster campaign, we came to understand that the Persil brand had always been about the role that washing plays in family life. And we realised that nearly 20 years had passed since we last asked the question, 'What does being a mother really mean today?' Our answer reflected the fact that, in the period between the 1960s and the 1980s, women had assumed a far more assertive and independent role in family life. This insight led not just to a great poster campaign for the old Persil powder, but to a whole new generation of Persil advertising.

But can something as simple as this five-step process really be infallible in delivering growth? ('Infallible', after all, was the word used in the introduction.) I believe it can, because the Five 'I's challenges some of the most dearly held but muddle-headed tenets of the marketing profession. To whet your appetite, here are five of the more surprising things the Five 'I's process throws up:

- All popular forms of market segmentation are inadequate, and a five-dimensional approach, which is apparently simpler, is more powerful.
- Brand positioning as a tool is much over-played and over-complicated.
- All marketing plans are fundamentally flawed and guarantee that at least half the money is wasted.
- The creative team should be briefed after the communications plan has been written, even though the whole trillion dollar industry is geared up to do it the other way round.
- Brand valuation is just part of a bigger approach to measuring and tracking brand health.

The Five 'I's also expose the simple things that so many companies get wrong. Here again are five of my favourites:

- Most strategies are too long-winded and the onward communication is woeful. You can't KISS but you can MISS – you can't keep it simple but you can make it simple, stupid.
- On the other hand, freedom of information and empowerment are both overdone. The vast majority of people in a business need to know the destination, their role in it and the incentive, but they do not need to know the full strategy.
- Most companies give up once an innovation is launched.
- Most companies plan in one-year cycles, even though impact nearly always takes more than a year.
- Media buying is dull, impact is interesting. CEOs will never take media seriously but they might take an interest in impact.

This is all simple to understand, but hard to do, just like sport. But then these days sport is more professional than business, and there is a better understanding of the need for strategy and implementation because the results, good or bad, are obvious and the sports teams or individuals really care about the outcome. You could say that business has just been made too complicated, and there seem to be too many apparently successful outcomes. But actually it is not that complex, and there is only one outcome that matters – profitable growth. In fact, it is obvious when businesses are achieving this and when they are not; as obvious as whether Manchester United is a better football team than Coventry City, or Australia is a better rugby team than Scotland, or Tiger Woods a better golfer than me.

So if it's all so obvious, let's find out how to make it happen.

CHAPTER 1

Insight

If you've ever felt your wallet for the price of a *risotto con tartufi* in a Turinese trattoria, you'll know that the white Italian truffle is one of the most overpriced foods on the planet. These famously stinky fungi often retail for around $450 per gram – so those few slivers you spotted in the rice were certainly worth their weight in gold. The main reason for their high price is that farming them is still beyond the ken of modern science. These subterranean fungi are maddeningly difficult to find, but their preferred habitat is beneath the roots of oak trees in the woods above the northern Italian town of Alba. For centuries, these hills have been stalked by secretive individuals, known as the *tartufai* – professional truffle hunters. To unearth their truffles, the *tartufai* employ a combination of insights – about the seasons, the weather, the terrain, the flora – along with an inspired assistant, the truffling pig, whose sense of smell is such that it can detect the precious fungi several feet below the ground. The *tartufai*'s reward for their strange occupation is to conjure a handsome living from a business that requires no investment, has no overheads, no expenditure and not even any physical assets, unless you count the pig, of course. Insight alchemy, indeed.

In many walks of life we see the rewards of rare and unusual combinations of insights. It's how the great novelist creates the compelling character. You can see it in the work of the political journalist who looks behind the headlines and briefings to tell you what is really going on. It's what happens when a close friend gives you a wonderful present that you would never have bought for yourself. And occasionally you find a really great marketer who has the insights that can generate serious top-line growth for your brand.

In recent years, insight has become a word much used – and misused – in marketing. By 'insight', we really mean a fresh, discerning, penetrating fact that, when combined with insights drawn from a wide variety of sources, inspires ideas and action. But marketing insight is rarely as sound as the instinct of the truffling pig. Indeed, of all the Five 'I's that go to make up great marketing, insight is the most elusive. But that doesn't mean that there aren't reliable methods of tracking it down. So in this chapter we'll look at five sources of insight and five research techniques that will bring you to within touching distance of that Eureka moment: when you unearth the truffle, find the gold nugget in your crucible or produce that pearl of marketing insight.

Just like hunting for truffles, one of the keys to finding marketing insight is to know what you want and to look for it in the right place. But unfortunately, a great deal of marketers' time and energy is wasted on false trails through the wrong terrain entirely. One of the most common ways for marketers to go astray is in the search for what are known as 'competitive insights' – the idea that a detailed understanding of your competitors will somehow miraculously transform your own business. Sadly, these 'competitive' insights are rarely anything of the sort. In fact, if you're ever in need of a pick-me-up at the end of a long week, just read a competitor's analysis of your own business. Forget the in-house criticism and bitching. Woolly? Opportunistic? Reactive? Not thought through? No way! Believe me, in the minds of your competitors, the most hastily dictated strategy document will appear as a marvel of Machiavellian intent. Of course, that doesn't mean that where you stand versus your competitors, both current and historic, is not a source of insight – but it certainly shouldn't be over-rated.

Competitive insight is not the only insight we bandy around. In fact, there's a blizzard of insight terminology to get lost in, much of which has nothing to do with real insight at all. More worryingly, the plethora of terms serves only to distract from a bigger and far more ghastly reality: the fact that for many people, insight has become almost synonymous with 'research' or 'consumer' insight.

Frankly, consumer research is so dangerous and so over-used that it should be given a health warning. This is not to say that understanding your consumers is not valuable, but it is nowhere near as valuable as people think, particularly when it is not complemented by other kinds of insight. Perhaps the problem starts with the word 'consumer'. The only true consumer is a shark who does nothing but eat and produce little sharks. But however much we want to think of people as 'consumers', they remain stubbornly human, and our precious brands play just a tiny part in their lives. Yet in research we so often forget this, and recruit people into focus groups and quantitative surveys largely on the basis of their consumption of our products – with little thought for what kind of people they really are. If we take so little time and trouble to understand our subjects, it's surely no wonder that their 'insights' are so often backward-looking and uninspiring. As Henry Ford put it so well, 'If I'd listened to my consumers, I'd have given them a faster horse.'

The shortcomings of consumer insight have not stopped market research agencies re-branding themselves 'consumer insight agencies' or market research managers re-titling themselves 'consumer insight managers'. It is true that there are an increasing number of more imaginative research techniques now available (and some of these will be covered in this chapter), but for the most part, focus groups and surveys are the dominant instruments of insight in marketing, and very blunt tools they are – far closer to the hammer than to the scalpel.

The truth is that most of what passes for an insight in marketing is really just a finding. What's the difference between the two? Let's imagine that we're profiling a person (not a consumer, mind) called John.

John is male, 28 years old, lives in a city and earns $100k a year as a manager working for a large firm.

These are findings: a set of socio-demographic facts about John from which we could infer relatively little. We might have found this out in a survey or in the warm-up at the start of a focus group. But let's continue:

John is the fourth of five brothers. Both parents had very successful careers as academics, a profession that all his four brothers have also pursued. But John chose a career in a large corporate bank, where he works long hours. He spends his money on status cars, and plays golf and does rock climbing when he has any spare time. He is single and unattached.

These too are findings that could have come from the same sources, but we are starting to build up a picture of the man rather than the statistic. We might assume he is ambitious and interested in money, because of the career he has chosen, which is very different from his parents and siblings. His hobbies might suggest that he is an individualistic, outdoor type, not averse to risk. But the profile is still patchy and very much inferred. We have yet to meet, observe or speak to John –

or indeed to anyone who knows him. We haven't looked at trends relating to people in his situation. We haven't analysed studies of large families or the implications of being the second youngest of such a large group of siblings. We may perhaps have begun to flesh out a picture based on our own personal experience of academics and corporate bankers, although this could just as easily be based on their representations in popular culture. So what's next?

John is totally driven to succeed. He is single and has few friends because he has real problems with relationships. He doesn't watch much TV, but reads certain speciality magazines. He buys Absolut vodka and likes to shop on the Internet, visiting an average of six sites on a regular basis. John also has a cocaine habit which is starting to put strains on his income, high though it is.

Now things are beginning to get a bit more interesting – and they should be. Marketers spend a lot of time and money finding out information like this – his consumption of media and brands, his shopping behaviour and use of the Internet. It's the kind of information that could come from surveys, meetings, observations, responses to open-ended questions about his feelings and attitudes, backed up perhaps by studies of trends, sociological studies and so on. The cocaine habit is certainly eye-catching – but do we have an insight yet? Afraid not, so let's read on.

John's younger brother is five years his junior. For five years John enjoyed the undivided attention of his parents and his elder brothers, then his younger brother arrived and went on to be brilliantly successful in everything he did.

Now if John had a therapist, she would be quick to point out that a lot of his behaviour – his choice of career, his relentless ambition, his failed relationships, his addiction (including his purchase of vodka) – could well stem from the fact that he has never come to terms with the sense of rejection he felt on the arrival and subsequent success of his younger brother. Well, that is an insight! And it's a very good one if you're trying to help John overcome his addiction or improve his love life. But it's not much use if you're trying to work out how he'll vote in the next election. It's not much help if you want to know what Christmas present to buy him. And from the point of view of a marketer – I'm afraid it's just another finding.

So what does all this tell us about insight? There are five lessons that can be learnt:

1. The value of an insight comes from the way it will be applied, so you need to know what you're looking for.

2. Insights can come from anywhere, so never restrict your sources. And remember that the most valuable insights are likely to come from a multiplicity of sources, not from one single source of inspiration.

3. Sometimes an insight can be inferred – and sometimes it is very simple. We could have got close to an insight about John that would explain his ambition or addiction from the first set of findings. But it requires a degree of tenacity to get a truly great insight.

4. If you know what you're looking for, you know when you've found it. That's what inspires action. If we had been John's therapist looking to help him with his addiction, we would have known instantly that the insight about his younger brother was the key, and we would have used this to give him the help he needed.

5. John might never have told you about his feelings towards his brother – so don't expect him to tell you all you need to know in a focus group or survey.

When we apply this to marketing, how do we know when we're basing our actions on findings rather than on true insight alchemy? The only real proof is in the sales figures, but it does no harm to look back and see some of the things that insight alchemy has achieved.

There was a time when all pet foods were sold in cans that looked the same. The assumption was that as animals can't talk and will eat most things, a wide choice of products was irrelevant. Certainly, the idea of a super premium offer in pet food seemed absurd. But this ignored the fact that some people really love their pets, almost as a surrogate child or lover – and they're quite happy to pay extra if they think they're buying what Tiddles or Fido really wants. A few years ago Mars Petfood realised that it was possible to make discernibly better pet food at an affordable on-cost and to package it in a far more attractive way, by using foil trays. These had appetite appeal for the owner, and because they were smaller, avoided the problem of unsightly half-eaten cans in the fridge. They also offered the potential for big improvements in profit margin, because the premium Mars could charge was considerably higher than the on-cost. This combination of insights – about people, the market and margin structure, technology and packaging – inspired the highly successful and profitable Cesar and Sheba brands. Mars found its insight because it was looking for more margin, and having segmented the market, it saw a better way to meet the needs of a segment of pet owners.

There was also a time when there was no differentiation in car insurance. It was a legal requirement and largely a grudge purchase, which was made worse by having to fill in forms and wait for insurance quotes and policies to be issued. Nor was there any profit. The lack of differentiation in the market meant that consumers bought on price, and over-supply had forced the prices down. Claims costs were also rising, as heavier traffic led to more accidents and people could afford more expensive cars to prang; both trends which were set to increase. Claims costs took up 70 per cent of the premium, and the remaining 30 per cent went on administration and the broker's commission. But an entrepreneur called Peter Woods spotted a flaw at the heart of the system. Customers were ringing brokers who often did little more than ring the insurance companies on their behalf. If he could persuade people to ring directly, he realised he could offer them 20–30 per cent discounts, and with the right software, he could actually fill out their forms for them, give them a quote and post it to arrive the following day. These insights – about the industry structure, trends, margins, people and the market – inspired Direct Line, the first UK telephone car insurance business. It quickly took 20 per cent of the market, and has gone on to become a general insurance and financial services business selling mortgages, pensions and life policies.

The most important feature of these examples of insight alchemy is that they inspired action. From this we can infer that those alchemists had a reason for looking for their insights, and that they knew where to look. After all, pigs know a truffle when they smell one, and their owners know the hills like the backs of their hands. But where should we marketers look for our marketing insight? Let's find out.

FIVE SOURCES OF INSIGHT

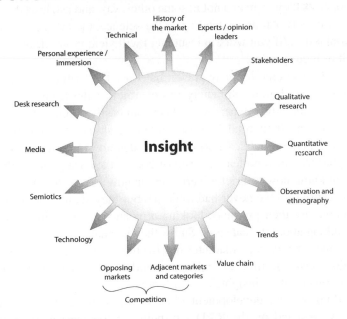

Figure 1.2 Sources of insight

There are actually so many sources of marketing insight, and so many techniques for tracking it down, that it's impossible to do them all justice – and also futile, since the sources and techniques are expanding the whole time. However, as the diagram shows, it is possible to identify some of the most consistently reliable and inspiring sources.

In this section of the chapter we're going to focus on five main areas:

1. Technical insight
2. History
3. Markets
4. Trends
5. Semiotics.

1. Technical insight

The single most powerful source of insight is technical insight – the craftsman-like understanding of how your product or service works and where it could be improved. Perhaps the most useful of all marketing exercises is to spend some time with the R&D department (or whatever the equivalent is in your business); simply ask the right questions and listen to the answers with an open mind. Find out how things work and how they were developed, learn why things were developed as they were and not in some other way, and ask how things could be done differently. An understanding of the science, the engineering or even the actuarial issues (if you work in insurance) will yield more ideas in a day than a month of focus groups.

Technicians come in many guises, but I use the term to refer to the people in a business who are ultimately responsible for developing the product or service that the buyer experiences. They can easily be identified by their love of proclaiming their total lack of marketing skills. 'Obviously I am not a marketing person, but …' normally precedes any fairly insightful comment from your technical colleagues. But of course they are good marketers. They may not know how to brief advertising, or how to develop a pricing strategy (just because they've never had to do it), but they spend a lot of time watching people use their products, looking at what the competitors are doing and just thinking about the category. Sadly, they normally have a better feel for the market than the average marketer has for the science. But the good marketer who does take the time to understand and listen can find extremely useful connections to other insights.

Working on the development of some premium differentiated fuels for Shell, we insisted on the R&D guy being in the workshop to develop the concepts. He began by telling us, 'But it is only 3 per cent better, no-one in a normal car in normal conditions would ever notice a difference.'

'Explain it to us,' we replied.

Having understood the science (well, roughly understood, to be fair), we were able to connect this to the people and the situations where that 3 per cent better really mattered – the situations where it was better for acceleration, or for the engine, or for the environment. These fuels are now on the market in various parts of the world, as Optimax in the UK and V Power in the Far East.

A seemingly simple project for Unilever to develop an ice lolly in a cardboard tube unearthed a trove of interesting properties of ice. Leading-edge research showed that ice could deliver fundamental properties of energy release, and new depths of hydration that could not be achieved by simply drinking liquids. The research also made it clear that ice has a 'play value' that a soft drink, however fizzy, simply cannot match. After all, with ice you can nibble it, lick it or roll it round your tongue – and you certainly can't do that with a can of cola; Calippo Shots was its first successful result. (It was subsequently rebranded Solero, but that's quite another story.) Calippo Shots were packs of small ice spheres that could be poured into the mouth and gave more refreshment. They allowed us to appeal to an older teen market, which was the marketing concept we were looking for, but for us the real insight came from the technical side.

Many years ago, while working on the account for Bell's whisky, I made the remarkable discovery that the United Distillers marketing team (as it was then) knew virtually nothing about their famous tipple. Why was it better than any of its rivals? Nobody could really say. Then, an inspirational master blender explained that Bell's tasted better than Famous Grouse because it contained a higher percentage of malts, which were better blended and, on average, older. The marketing team latched on to the age factor, which had often been used as a selling point for pure malts, but had never been used to sell blended whiskies before. This insight led to the relaunch of Bell's, highlighting the age factor that is still featured both on the pack and in the advertising today.

Looking at things from the technical point of view can also reveal some surprising marketing opportunities. When the R&D teams were developing liquids for washing machines, they insisted that the only effective way of using them was via a dispenser. From a marketing perspective, this at first appeared to be a serious obstacle, as it would mean asking customers not just to accept the idea of a liquid but also to change the whole way that they used their machines. The marketing team at Procter, however, chose to see this as an opportunity. They gave their dispenser a snappy name – the Arielette – and used it to highlight the modernity of their product and its improved efficacy.

There are no specific techniques or tools to recommend here, just three pieces of advice.

- Invest the time to understand.
- Involve the technicians as much as possible and make sure they know what you know so they can help you make connections.
- Listen generously. The solution they're offering may not be people-friendly but ask yourself two questions. Could it be adapted? Or – could we make a virtue out of the apparent problem?

2. History

One of the best, most simple and most insightful pieces of analysis is to draw a graph of the market and the shares of the key brands over a 10, 20 or 30 year time-frame. Observe the major changes in either market size or relative share, and find out what happened. To give a quick idea of what this would reveal, here are three impressionistic sketches of the major changes in three very different markets.

Salty Snacks UK

In fairly recent memory, companies in the British salty snacks category used to offer a wide portfolio of snacks, but then the relaunch of Walker's crisps as a power brand gave the market a serious jolt. There followed product innovation in the form of new flavours and new products, like Dorito's corn chips, and with the launch of Pringles, a new kind of product based on new benefits such as reward and indulgence.

Beer Market USA

The American beer market kicked off in 1933 when President Roosevelt remarked that it was 'a good time for a beer' and promptly repealed prohibition. At first there was a focus on regional breweries and local brands, but gradually the big national brewers rolled out countrywide. Product innovation came in the form of lites, and then new competition arrived from new sources such as imports and microbreweries.

Insurance UK

The insurance industry really took off with the explosion of home ownership. We can then observe several changes of distribution channel as the industry moved from direct sales force (the Man from the Pru) to intermediary (brokers) and from intermediary to direct telephone selling (Direct Line). More recently we've seen product bundling, as insurance is increasingly sold as part of a more comprehensive financial package.

This kind of 50,000 feet view changes your perspective on a market, and reminds us of some timeless truths, for example, (surprise, surprise) that the introduction of new benefits changes markets. But it also gives some insights that are peculiar to each market: for example, that historically financial services have been channel-driven.

What these insights lead to depends on what you're looking for, but here are some insights that could be gleaned from this kind of exercise:

- Could Golden Wonder or United Biscuit not have spotted what Walker's dramatic refocus on one power brand was doing to the market and responded?
- Could any of the established beer companies not have anticipated Smirnoff Ice? And what will they do if or when marijuana is legalised?
- Could the big financial services businesses not have leveraged the Internet better and more quickly? (Some, like Prudential in the UK, did, to be fair.)

When looking for historical insight, here are three pieces of advice:

- Go back into history to get some perspective and some inspiration.
- Analyse the structural changes in your market.
- Talk to the people who were there if at all possible.

3. Markets

Markets – all markets – are invaluable sources of insight. As we'll see in this section, that insight can be unlocked by asking three straightforward questions:

- What can be learnt by comparing markets in adjacent – or in very different – areas?
- What assumptions does everyone in the market make?
- What is the market profitability, and where is value captured in the value chain?

So let's find out what some of the answers are.

Comparing markets

The mainstay of the consulting profession is the ability to cross-reference different markets, both product and geographic. There are never any precise comparisons and the circumstances are always slightly different, but there is always insight. Sometimes the insight is easy to grasp, particularly if it's from an adjacent category, but you can also find inspiration by contrasting seemingly unconnected markets.

First, let's see what can be learnt from a fairly obvious cluster of markets – ice cream, confectionery, salty snacks and soft drinks. Marketers in any one of these categories would get huge insights by looking at these five areas in the adjacent markets:

- Benefits or needs – which are dominant and which are growing?
- Segmentation – what are the clusters of product types, occasions, places and people involved in these markets, and how do they interrelate? (This is the 'Who? What? Why? When? Where?' approach which we'll be looking at in detail later in the chapter.)
- Portfolio – what portfolio approach is being used, with what results? Are there lots of stand-alone brands, or is there a trend towards fewer bigger brands that address similar benefits but in a variety of formatted solutions?
- Pricing – how are the adjacent markets structured in terms of price segments? Is it all mainstream, or are economy, premium or super premium segments emerging?
- Communications/connectivity – how are they getting their message across?

So what insights could marketers have gathered by answering these questions? Here are a few simple examples:

- Ice cream went super premium ahead of all the other categories, although most of them are now following.
- Red Bull and isotonic drinks introduced new functional benefits that have transformed the soft drinks market and will eventually transform the others. For example, energy confectionery bars are already appearing. (Mars bars seem to have gone for a strategy offering more indulgence, but could they be the original functional energy food in need of updating?)
- Coke pioneered the route to market innovation with vending machines

and draught Coke for cafes and bars – approaches that all the other categories have learnt from.

- Cadbury's has a very successful theme park called Cadbury's World. Coke has used sponsorship to build international fame and ubiquity. Companies need to think laterally to build market presence.
- There is a gifting segment in confectionery but there is none in the other categories, although there is some evidence that it could emerge.
- Soft drinks and ice cream have taken very different approaches to distribution and portfolio strategy. Ice cream makers have traditionally focused on two main channels of distribution: fridges which they own and install in the local store, or franchised mobile fridges (the old 'Stop me and buy one' idea). Soft drinks companies like Coca-Cola, on the other hand, have had a distribution strategy that ensured their drinks were available wherever you turned. This meant that soft drinks firms were quick to grab the chance of 'pouring rights' in burger chains like McDonald's, while the ice cream firms missed out and allowed McDonald's ice cream to become one of the biggest selling brands in the world.

So far we have only looked at a set of clearly adjacent markets or categories. But great insight can also be found through comparisons that are far less obvious. We must remember that great insight has to be sought with a purpose, so let's think about some problems facing various industries and look for comparisons in a few unexpected places.

Problem: Judging by the mutual bitching that goes on between car manufacturers and their dealer networks, channel marketing in cars is ripe for some innovation.
Comparison: Financial services were channel-focused but are now developing multi-channel strategies; perhaps this might offer some clues.

Problem: As the difference between banks and insurance companies becomes increasingly blurred, financial services businesses now need to manage portfolios of brands that increasingly overlap.
Comparison: This has been the case in South Africa for some time, where companies like Nedcor and Old Mutual have successfully handled different brands of both banks and insurance companies. Fast moving consumer goods businesses have been tackling this issue for decades, so they could also offer useful insights.

Problem: Fast moving consumer goods cannot seem to make the old 60/40 above and below the line model work any more.

Comparison: For many years India has used events marketing to great effect. Companies like Unilever have regularly staged roadshows that bring their products to towns and villages across the country.

Problem: Retailers need to innovate but they have no conventional R&D function.
Comparison: How do pharmaceuticals manage R&D to develop marketplace innovation? What is changing in retail in Japan?

Problem: Pharmaceutical companies have to manage brands sold over the counter based on products that also have to be marketed to the professionals (the doctors who must endorse them).
Comparison: How do car companies do this? How does Chinese medicine, the oldest pharmaceutical industry in the world, work?

Market comparisons, then, are a quick and extremely effective way of gaining insight. and certainly shouldn't be the sole preserve of the management consultants.

Market assumptions

Another extremely valuable exercise is to look at the assumptions that every-one in the market makes and then to challenge them. Here are a few simple examples of how marketers have done this, with spectacular success.

Assumption: Mini-vans are not meant to be pretty or easy to drive.
Challenge: Renault's launch of the elegant Espace led to the creation of a whole new category in cars – the people carrier.

Assumption: Soft drinks are for teenagers. Taste and refreshment are the only benefits.
Challenge: Snapple and Red Bull have successfully challenged this by target-ing adults and young adults, offering the benefits of well-being and energy.

Assumption: Certain financial services need to be sold face to face.
Challenge: Hardly any financial services need to be sold face to face, though some people still prefer this method, and some direct selling is supported with a human contact for certain stages of the process.

Assumption: Shaving is a male category.
Challenge: Gillette spotted this was untrue before anyone else and built a

whole new market, much to the relief of millions of men who no longer had to share their razors with their wives or girlfriends.

Assumptions: Hotels should have a nice reception, lounges and restaurants on the ground floor. No one wants to spend the night next to a motorway.
Challenge: Formule 1 is a chain of hotels that is famous across France, and increasingly in other countries. They offer the bare minimum in terms of food and beverages, front of house and general service, and they're built right next to motorways. But the check-in is rapid, the rooms are adequately comfortable and they are very cheap. It is an excellent example of re-segmenting a market: by targeting the value-conscious motorist they totally redesigned the conventional hotel.

Of course there are as many examples of brands that fail because they enter a category without understanding the category rules. But if you can understand how a market works in terms of the five factors already listed – benefits, segmentation (including route to market or distribution), portfolio, pricing and communications – and systematically challenge each one, there are some great insights to be found.

Market profitability and the value chain

Analysing the value chain means working back from a product's purchase price to the raw materials, and working out where value is created and captured along the way. Management consultants are particularly good at this kind of analysis, and it can clearly reveal what accounts for the profitability of a market. Certainly, all marketers should know the cost structure of their brands. If you don't, just draw two columns. In the left, list the benefits in order of importance to people, and in the right, list the costs of providing each, just roughly.

Some of the examples quoted earlier show how a simple sum on the back of the smallest envelope could have been used to give some useful insights. Peter Woods of Direct Line realised that 30 per cent of the price of car insurance went on administration and the broker, and saw a chance to set up a business that cut out the intermediary. It would also not have required a financial wizard to figure out that the biggest cost of building a hotel is in the ground floor facilities, which are not valued by the weary traveller just looking for a bed for the night.

My favourite example of this type of analysis is a simple insight gained by Campbell's Soup in the United States, which had a huge impact. An initial piece of analysis revealed that chicken noodle soup was a major line for the company, actually more important than it had first realised, which was itself an insight into its portfolio of products. The research also showed that people preferred chicken with the noodles rather than just a spoonful of noodles. This presented a clear opportunity, as Campbell's knew that at relatively little cost, it could increase the amount chicken relative to the noodles. This was used as the basis of a relaunch which drove sales by 10 per cent in a static market. It was beautifully promoted in an ad showing the youngest brother of a big Italian family getting some chicken in his soup for the first time in his life, when the bowl finally came round to him.

So again, we can see that it is possible to find insights from a quick analysis requiring no more than a pen, a piece of paper and a little bit of imagination.

4. Trends

There is a fun game you can play with names. Take the name of your first pet and your mother's maiden name and put them together to make the name of porn star, or take your father's middle name, the name of your road and the number of children or siblings to make the name of a US president. In my case I get Sammy Eglinton and Herbert Ormond IV.

So what game was it that came up with Faith Popcorn as a futurologist? No disrespect is intended here. There is real value in standing back and trying to understand what the trends are and how this might impact your market and your brands. Since Faith Popcorn in the United States and the Henley Centre in Europe first came onto the scene, there are now multitude of people and agencies who, for a fee, will help you get in touch with the zeitgeist. Who predicted that, one wonders? Techniques vary, from sniff the air, smell the coffee and watch the stars to the deeply analytical.

At Added Value we recently produced a summary of all the mega global trends. It was put together using studies we had conducted for clients, studies done by others that clients had shared with us, and some fresh semiotic work on youth culture. Figure 1.3 is what we came up with.

Now here is the rub. What do you do with this to take it from 'Gee whizz' to 'Aha! Yes!'? This is where the brilliance of the name Faith Popcorn comes in. If like me you enjoy popcorn, you will know it is deeply pleasurable while you are eating it but leaves no lasting impression. Whereas with faith, a trust in the heart not just the head, you can change the world.

What you do with these studies is this. Write down the top five strategic issues you face, in short simple sentences. Take your top team and discuss each trend in relation to your market and your issues. Then make a judgement call. You cannot respond to every trend; you may have noticed some are virtually

Trends	Change over time	Today	Brands that are riding the trends
Informality	Formality to fit in → Formality as status → Universal informality	Blurring of boundaries Informality	The Gap
Intensity	Post-war striving → Rebellion → Discovery → Adrenalin	Seeking physical stimulation Cynicism requiring escapism	Playstation
Wellbeing quest	Enduring illness → Curing illness → Preventing illness → Health	Seeking health & vitality Understanding of mind–body–spirit needs Social responsibility	The Positive Food Company (Mars)
Global interdependence	Institutions (nationalism) → The company good → Growth for wealth (profit first) → Anti-trust (holistic view)	Sense of the individual as a 'world citizen' 'Global train' of interconnectedness	Body Shop
Simplification	Focus on tradition → Focus on new knowledge → Focus on control → Focus on simplicity	Over-information, driving a sense of vulnerability Seeking simple choices	First Direct
Nostalgia	Focus on present → Focus on future → Focus on present reality → Focus on past	Romanticising the past Desire for familiarity and security Search for authenticity and realness	New Mini
Premium reward culture	Restraint → Guilty indulgence → Permissible indulgence	'I deserve it' indulgence Compensatory behaviour Mainstreaming of the premium	L'Oreal
Individuality	Confirm (institution) → Shock (anti-institution) → Status (hierarchy) → Bond (community) → Expression (individual)	A rejection of the formulaic Master of my own destiny 'The individual' as nucleus Reinvention and rejuvenation of self	Swatch
Affinity communities	Geographic (physical) → Workplace → Activity based → Attitude (virtual)	Multi-identified individuals Growth in virtual working and living Lifestyle clusters	Vodafone
Technology commodity	Technology as hobby → Technology as status → Technology as hero → Technology as commodity	Integrating technology into everyday life Gaming as 'the new football' – cornerstone of on-line communities	Nokia

Figure 1.3 The trends

contradictory. All you can do is drill down into one or at most two, and decide you are going to use them as an insight to inspire an idea and some innovation.

It's not easy to give simple examples of people doing this in the past. Their actions would be linked to insight alchemy, not simply to a reaction to one identified trend.

Going back to the trends, let's pick just one, well-being, to show the kind of action it could inspire in two very different industries: food and financial services. Within well-being there is a stark development. Within a matter of a few years, significant numbers of people across the world will have been genetically coded. They will know with a high degree of certainty what will kill them unless something unnatural happens.

The food industry increasingly knows the link between certain types of foods and the prevention of certain serious ailments. Right now, the message is sinking in that we must eat five portions of fruit and veg every day, and governments are actually promoting it. This will get more sophisticated and individualized, as sure as God made little apples, presumably for some purpose. This insight should be inspiring some very urgent innovations if it is not already doing so.

Insurance companies have a right to ask for a medical before issuing life policies, but legislation is currently preventing the financial services industry from using genetic information to discriminate against high risk individuals. How long can this hold? If a company knows with much greater accuracy the life expectancy of potential customers, how can this not affect its behaviour towards them? Surely this insight should be prompting businesses to develop different types of mortgages, investments and insurance products?

Trends, if used properly and selectively, are a very high octane source of insight. Depending on your philosophy or religion, you believe either that we are trying to plug into the inevitable, or that forewarned is forearmed to change the future.

One of my favourite quotes is the following:

In order to grow, you have to have a point of view about the future...

To this we always add:

... and the only way to predict the future is to shape it.

5. Semiotics

In Added Value we rebranded semiotics, 'Decoder', not because it makes it any easier to explain but because just the word 'semiotics' caused clients' eyes to glaze over. Since we have found semiotics to be one of the most powerful forms of insight, we have worked hard to demystify it, with limited success. Nevertheless, the fact remains that semiotics can remain opaque until you see the output.

Let me explain. It is worth it because the truth that underlies semiotics is actually the root cause of why businesses find the Five 'I's process so hard. Our brains are wired to detect and act upon patterns. Pavlov proved this by ringing bells at his dogs' feeding time, and 'Pavlovian response' is now part of the vernacular. Without patterns in our mind we cannot survive. You picked up this book and are reading it because it looks like a book and it obeys the conventions of a book: title, author, cover, pages, words, page numbers and so on. It might have been a sandwich, they can do amazing things with food and colourants. But, no, you were right, it is a book. Our brains could not function without patterns that allow us to make decisions and to free up the space to process new information as it comes along. Animals are completely dominated by these patterns; fortunately, we are not. But we are more influenced than we might admit.

These patterns affect every aspect of our lives. This explains racism. Consider these three statements: Italians are excitable; the Irish are wild and poetic; black people rob you. All three are racist statements, and the last is obviously the most offensive and wrong. However, some misguided people hold this view because they have detected a pattern and misinterpreted it. Poor people who live next to rich people with no hope of ever attaining their advantages legally, tend to commit crimes. In sociology it is known as the theory of alienation, and it applies and has applied to any race.

However, I find it fairly easy to support the first statement. Italians *are* excitable. They are passionate, quick to lose their temper, but just as quick to hug and make up. They talk very fast and wave their arms about. Unless you are Italian, and even if you are, you are probably nodding along to this. These observations are given with affection by a self-conscious uptight Brit. They are of course just a pattern many of us have formed in our minds. Where did it come from? It comes in part from personal experience, but I have not met that many Italians, certainly not a statistically robust sample, and those I know I approached with a pattern already partially formed in my head. I was looking for certain behaviours. I was looking for Sophia Loren. And that explains where the patterns really come from. They are culturally rooted – in the case of Sophia, rooted in popular culture. To emphasise this point, think of colours. Purple means luxury in some cultures, but is the colour of death in others, while in western countries a red cross is associated with medical assistance.

Semiotics is the study of culturally rooted codes or patterns, by which we interpret and upon which we act. Semiotic insight enables us to decode the codes. In fact it does more; it allows us to see trends. As the grim example of the codes of racism showed, patterns are hard to change, but they can and thankfully do evolve. If you decode the patterns, you can detect what is residual (that is, still present but becoming less relevant), what is current and what is emerging.

Brands are of course a pattern in the minds of people. Most brand purchases are made at a subconscious level, and brands help us by simplifying choice. Can you imagine the supermarket shopping trip if every purchase had to be appraised from first principles – do I like real fruit in my cereal or not? We would be there all day. At the risk of a sexist comment based on a culturally rooted pattern relating to the role of women in relation to men, have you ever noticed how much longer it takes a man to shop for groceries, or how long it takes a woman to shop for clothes?

The actual pattern relating to a brand – its packaging or presentation, the market itself – is very influential and can be decoded. We feel a certain way about financial services and we interact with them in a certain way because of an 'iceberg' pattern. An iceberg pattern means that some of these feelings are visible, but most are way below the surface. They are the result of every interaction we have ever had involving the financial services industry. That means every TV show and comedian we have seen that referred to bankers, every article we have ever read about banks mistreating small businesses or Third World debt, every bank fascia we see in the high street, the language banks use in their statements, the people we knew at school that became bankers, every mistake they've ever made, every loan they turned down ... oh yes, and also what they say in their advertising. Banks were sorely disappointed when they started advertising and changing their branches to look more like shops, because people still did not trust them. It is changing now, and new patterns and codes in financial services are at last emerging.

Appendix 1, written by Michael Harvey and Dr Malcolm Evans, gives a fascinating case study and exposes a little more of the black art of semioticians, for however hard one tries, it remains impossible fully to explain how outstanding semioticians do what they do. My favourite of Malcolm's semiotic insights was part of the alchemy that created a new range of soups for Campbell's which had the convenience of a can but all the freshness cues of a home-made product. Malcolm's whole presentation, which explained soup's role in various cultures both Western and Asian, was fascinating. We had already noticed that the soups in France that Campbell's had recently acquired were successful in part because they used the same packaging as UHT milk, a category that had patterns of freshness entrenched in people's minds. Malcolm nailed the reason that canned soups could never bridge the perceived fresh taste gap with home-made, however good the recipe. 'Canned soup is dead food', he said, and like all great insights everyone knew instantly that he was right – and what we should do about it.

Here are the five areas where semiotic analysis, or Decoder, can be used to best effect for growth insights:

- When working with a group of people (especially young people), in order to understand their passions and emerging trends.
- When analysing a market or category, to see below what is apparently a cluster of very different brands saying different things. Decoder can also help us to understand the conventions they are all following, and what might be challenged.
- When considering a brand in the context of its own market or in the context of other adjacent markets.
- When reviewing communications. Decoder allows you to see the residual, current and emerging codes of communication, and to detect the main platforms of brand positioning, as well as spot trends and gaps.
- When thinking about packaging and presentation. Since almost all innovation relies on breaking the accepted codes of presentation for that category (think of the iMac, Renault Espace, Pringles or Snapple), it helps to know the rules you are breaking.

So far in this chapter, we have covered technical insight, history, markets, trends and semiotics, and you'll have noticed that it's been a good few pages since any mention was made of the marketing industry's most favoured tool – consumer research. That's because the five sources of insight that have been focused on are all more powerful and effective than consumer insight, and they should be done ahead of, or at least alongside, any consumer research.

After all, doctors do not rely on their patients to make their diagnosis. They too use science, history, and understanding of particular branches of medicine, trends and patterns. However, they are also taught how to observe, question and prod patients, and use the information they get from this as a crucial part of their assessment and cure.

Perhaps now would be a good time to start prodding the patient to see what insights we get.

FIVE RESEARCH TECHNIQUES

All marketing research, just like all medical research, is ultimately research into people. In marketing, this research falls into two broad categories: exploration

– the search for growth insights – and evaluation – the verification that the applied insight is working. It is not quite as black and white as this, we verify as we learn and we learn as we verify, but it is a useful perspective. Figure 1.4 summarises the research diamond and the most common techniques used for exploration and evaluation.

At the insight stage of the Five 'I's process, we are concerned with

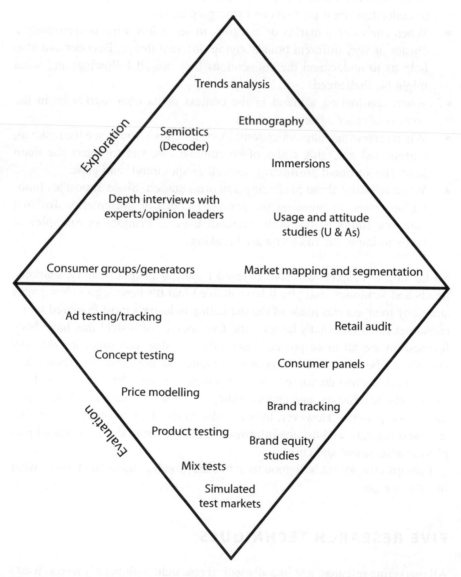

Figure 1.4 The research diamond

exploration. Investment return will cover the evaluation. We are not going to go through every technique, but again we'll focus on five approaches that have reliably delivered great insights:

1. Immersion or ethnographic research
2. Using experts and opinion leaders
3. Trade-offs and the Calibrator
4. Consumer generators
5. Segmentation or market mapping.

By now, you shouldn't be surprised to see that we won't be dealing with focus groups in any great detail. To be fair, focus groups may occasionally yield some enlightenment – but only if there is a very high quality brief and a really excellent moderator. But even then, there is only so much that can be discussed and learnt in a couple of hours.

And learning is what research is all about. Not necessarily learning in the schoolroom sense, but learning in the sense of these five words:

> **L**ook
> **E**xperience
> **A**sk
> **R**eview
> **N**umbers

Start by 'looking'. This is such an obvious statement that it might not seem worth saying. But too often there is a feeling that the real research only starts when we have some hapless researcher in front of the screen delivering the debrief. Believe me, the real research starts when you really start looking.

One of my favourite books on 'looking' is Desmond Morris' *Manwatching,* the follow-up to the best-selling *The Naked Ape*. It was based on visits he had made to 15 countries, where he observed different customs, habits and behaviours. Twenty-five years on it still makes fascinating reading. There is an excellent section on body piercing, at the time an emerging trend in punk culture, where he explains the importance of body mutilation involving pain as a way of bonding to a tribe. Having recently been to Ozzy Osbourne's rock festival I can see what he means.

The kind of research that Morris did is far more difficult to do than it might at first appear. That's because observation can influence the observed – I felt a little conspicuous at Ozfest – and you will sometimes need to get the right kind of urban guerrillas to go to certain places for you to collect video footage. I saw a film produced by one such dedicated group who had been to the townships of South Africa, where they talked to young guys about sunglasses. One thing that struck me was that the sunglasses were on their heads and not in front of their eyes for a lot of the time. Are sunglasses designed with this in mind, I wondered? Perhaps Oakleys are. But when you buy sunglasses, the mirrors in the shop are set up to show what they look like on your nose, not on your head. A simple yet very actionable insight.

Another thing occurred to me. Were the guys in the township aware of this behaviour? Perhaps not, or at least not until prompted. And even then, you cannot rely on people to tell you what they do and why they do it. It is not that they lie, although they sometimes do; it is simply that they are not aware of it or of its significance. One of the growth insights for Calippo, that brand of ice lolly in a tube of cardboard, was gained simply by watching young teens eat them, play with them and joke about them with a degree of innuendo. It's by looking, not by listening that you find out what's really happening.

The next step in LEARN is clear. 'Experience' it yourself. A good friend (now the chairman of a large foods business, so I hope he still recalls this) was presenting a proposal to invest a small amount of money to improve the opening mechanism for a pack of detergent of which he was then brand manager. His marketing director was not impressed with the research findings, believing that they did not justify the on-cost. In frustration, my friend passed the director the pack and said, 'Go on then, you open it.' Ten minutes later, with bloodied fingers (after a secretary had been summoned to bring scissors), the aperture was still too small to permit enough detergent to wash a hanky, and the marketing director conceded that the opening could do with some improvement. My friend's proposal was approved.

When you have looked and experienced, you'll be in a much better position to 'Ask' – to ask informed questions that will stimulate genuinely insightful responses. Then 'Review' what you have learnt and start to cross-reference with the insights you have gained from elsewhere.

The last letter, N, is for 'Numbers'. It is the last stage of the process because quantitative research should, as a general rule, calibrate the known. Doing the numbers bit first is a recipe for disaster. A very large (but not the largest) soft drinks manufacturer commissioned a usage and attitude study in the UK using a questionnaire it had developed in the United States. The findings were useless and downright perplexing until we had gone back and done the basic qualitative groundwork to put them in context, a process that was expensive and time consuming.

So if you want to learn, LEARN.

1. Immersion

The first two steps in LEARN, looking and experiencing, are often called immersion, or more correctly 'ethnographic research'. To really immerse yourself in your brand audience, you'll need some pre-research, a plan and also a guide. For this reason many marketers will brief outside people to help, and there are increasingly specialists who can do this. These specialists tend to focus on youth, because this is a key audience and because marketers are not always as young as their target audience, and things change fast. As you go through the immersion process, create a war room, where you put up all the memorabilia – your observations and insights, as well as other photos and souvenirs. By holding your meetings in the war room, you can stay within touching distance of your sources of insight and inspiration.

In immersion you should be interested in five main aspects of your current or intended audience's lives. These five aspects are what you should observe, experience (if possible) and hopefully understand. Here's a checklist of questions to think about.

Work	What do they do? How do they feel about what they do?
	How does it relate to the rest of their lives?
	Is it integral or peripheral, a means or an end?
Play	Where do they hang out?
	What do they watch or listen to?
	Who do they hang out with?
Events	What are the significant events in their lives?
	What provides structure?
	What do they look forward to or dread?
Relationships	What network of relationships do they have?
	How interrelated are they?
	What kind of relationships do they have with partners, and with authority?
Passions	What are they passionate about – sport, technology, music, mates, issues, causes?

However good your checklist, immersion is not a technique that lends itself to a highly systematic or scientific approach. One of the hardest projects I ever worked on was for a chain of holiday camps in the UK called Pontin's. Mr Pontin, like his contemporary Mr Butlin, had an insight in the post-war years about the working man's need for a week's holiday for a week's wages. He bought up redundant military bases and converted them to holiday camps. By 1995 they were looking very jaded, and we were tasked with coming up with some big idea to rejuvenate the brand, but without the bene-fit of being able to recommend what was really needed – a gazillion pounds' worth of investment. They were being upgraded but slowly, and we had to work with a product that was still a bit shabby.

I could not get my head into this one. I went off for a week with a colleague and we stayed in three of the camps. It was awful. But we stuck at it, we videoed lots of stuff, hung out in the bars, joined in the quiz nights, ate the fish and chips, watched the men get pissed and play pool and the women doll themselves up for the talent night. At an intellectual level we were beginning to immerse ourselves in the people who went to these places. Neither of us came from working class families but neither had we come from privileged backgrounds. We could remember family holidays that had been done on a shoestring because that was all our parents could afford, and more extravagant holidays in later years when money was more available. And we realised that, as kids, we did not differentiate and thoroughly enjoyed both. But I still did not get it.

A week later, on a public holiday, I dragged my kids along to another Pontin's camp. My overwhelming conclusion was that Pontin's was too far behind. Even the motorway service station where we stopped was better kitted out and had better food and facilities than this camp. I drove away from the camp in a bit of a grump, then my six-year-old son said, 'That was great. Can we go again, and next time can we stay?'

The penny dropped. Kids don't notice the bad stuff, just the freedom, the fun and the time you spend with them. And if you are a worker from a small industrial town, who does not spend as much time with your kids as you know you should, having somewhere you can afford to take them, where you can still get pissed and play pool, but they get to run around and have fun for a week, where at least you all go swimming together and have a laugh at the quiz night and where they get to stay up late…. All this makes you a better dad – and not much different from me, who had, after all, taken his kids on a rare public holiday to a place he thought was terrible but he happened to be working on. Not the most brilliantly original insight for a holiday camp, but the whole relaunch of Pontin's was focused on the kids. Sadly, one insight does not a turnaround make.

2. Using experts and opinion leaders

If you really want a bit of excitement, just bring a group of experts and opin-ion leaders together, put them in the right room, and create the right kind of free-thinking environment. Then, having thought through the areas you want to cover, toss the issues into the room in the form of big open-ended questions.

The effect is like a shoal of piranha round a juicy steak; and the output, in terms of marketing insight, is staggering.

In research for Levi's Engineered Jeans, a group was assembled that included DJs, youth and trend magazine editors, fashion designers, university lecturers, people who worked in clubs and bars, artists, musicians and writers, as well as sociologists and psychologists. They proved to be the easiest of groups to moderate because they were experts and all had opinions they were only too keen to share. The insights that they produced were crucial to the brand's success.

The case of Levi's Engineered Jeans was presented to the Market Research Society of Great Britain in 2002 on behalf of the client by Flemming from Thygesen and Paul McGowan from Added Value. (The paper is reproduced in full in Appendix 2.) In the study Paul and Flemming explain how they segmented the youth market and used this understanding to create a model of cascading influence and adoption of ideas from the leading edge group, which they named 'Cultural creatives, Modernists and Edge' to the more mainstream groups, 'Fashion flirts, Labellists and Regulars'. This was a very detailed and thorough study, but for any market it is relatively easy to locate the opinion leaders within your target audience.

The simplest technique is to start with an individual in the target group and get the names of his or her closest friends. Ask each of them who they all listen to about various subjects. You may find they all turn to one friend for tips on, say, computers, but another for advice on music. By cross-referencing the information, it is easy to identify who are the shakers and movers for the category you are interested in. Often one member of the group is clearly the most wired about everything. These are the people you want to talk to, but probably in smaller groups than a conventional focus group, or individually – or indeed both.

There is a cost attached to this in terms of both time and money. It can either take longer, or you may end up talking to fewer people in a given time, and there is a financial cost premium of at least 100 per cent. But the output is 10 times, sometimes 1000 times, more insightful than the kind you get from a conventional focus group. In work we did for Frito Lay, we assembled a group comprising the editor of a music magazine, a journalist for a PC gaming magazine, a youth fashion expert, a semiotic consultant and a psychologist who was running a study into self-esteem in teenagers. In three hours we came away with more inspiration for innovation, brand communications and distribution than six months of conventional research and market analysis would have yielded.

In the two examples given here, Levi's and Frito Lay, the emphasis was on the young, which is not surprising given the nature of these markets. What may be surprising is that with only a very few exceptions, I believe the emphasis should always be on the young. Even in markets more evenly spread in terms of demographics, the most interesting insights come from the younger person. For example, 80 per cent of all brand switching in beer happens below the age of 25. Even in financial services or retail, the most useful data for growth insights comes from down the age scale.

Younger people have opinions, their behaviour and attitudes are forming, they often have high disposable income, they go out more, and most importantly, they are the mainstream of tomorrow. And sad though it may be, as a 46-year-old I want to buy stuff that appeals to a 25-year-old, an age which I still am in my head.

3. Trade-offs and the Calibrator

Marketing, like business and life, is based on trade-offs. As Rosabeth Moss Kanter says in *When Giants Learn To Dance*:

> *Be sure you know every detail of your business – but delegate more responsibility to others.*

> *Be entrepreneurial and take risks – but don't cost the business anything by failing.*

> *Succeed, succeed, succeed – and raise terrific children.*

Weighing up the pros and cons is part of any business decision, but in marketing, the insight is gained from understanding which benefits people are prepared to trade off and in which situations they're prepared to do so. The problem is that you can't rely on people to tell you which trade-offs are acceptable to them. Henry Ford's quote – 'If I'd listened to my consumers, I'd have given them a faster horse' – is not quite accurate. If he'd really listened to his consumers, he would have found they wanted a horse that was incredibly fast, easy to keep, never got sick, didn't eat too much, was comfortable to ride, lived for 100 years, cost 5 cents, but still had a high resale value.

Brands are always a compromise, and for this reason needs trade-offs should always form part of any study. As we'll see when we come to segmentation, it is particularly important to analyse trade-offs in different segments of your market. But there is one problem. Conventional trade-off studies are expensive and complex. In fact they are expensive because they are complex; they take up a lot of time in a quantitative questionnaire, for example. But although you should start with qualitative research, this is one area where you will need numbers.

Added Value solved this problem by developing a technique called Calibrator. It is divinely simple and therefore cheap and easy to use, which means it can be employed more often. It also takes up far less time than conventional trade-off analysis, and so can be used as part of a suite of research tools, by being embedded in surveys of usage and attitude or work assessing concepts, for example. The starting point for Calibrator has to be the right list of needs, and this can be gained from good market understanding, using some or all of the insight techniques listed, including conventional focus groups. The output should be a list of no more than 30 needs representing both existing needs and emotional needs that are as yet untapped.

The research then presents people with the needs grouped in threes. The order and groupings are rotated across the sample so every need can be compared with all the others in a statistically representative way. People are asked to ring the benefit that is most important to them in each group of three. On the law of averages any one benefit should be chosen one third of the time, and so the variance tells you the relative importance. Figures 1.5 a and b show typical output.

Unlike a simple ranking by order of importance, Calibrator shows you how people make trade-offs, as well as delivering a more sensitive hierarchy of people's 'top of the mind' priorities. But remember, it only tells you what people claim to be important to them, and there will be other factors that influence their brand preference. For example, choosing an airline that won't crash is pretty crucial, but it is unlikely to be a factor in brand choice as all airlines perform similarly when judged against this criterion. So it is always important to look at the Calibrator in conjunction with other measures of influence.

4. Consumer generators

Should we ever use focus groups? Can we ever talk about consumers in the context of insight? Sort of.

Focus groups comprising buyers – all right, let's use the 'c' word, consumers – of a brand give responses that require real expertise to interpret. Many a time a client will come away from a focus group convinced that a particular idea is of limited appeal because most people rejected it, or believing a particular idea is strongly held because most people agreed with it, only to be told by the moderator that neither is true. What people say and what they actually believe, what they really do and what they might do, are not the same thing. The good moderator essentially spots this from the most common and most important form of communication: body language. Yes, most of the group rejected the idea, but one or two really loved it, and as they became more passionate about it, you could see this having an effect on the others.

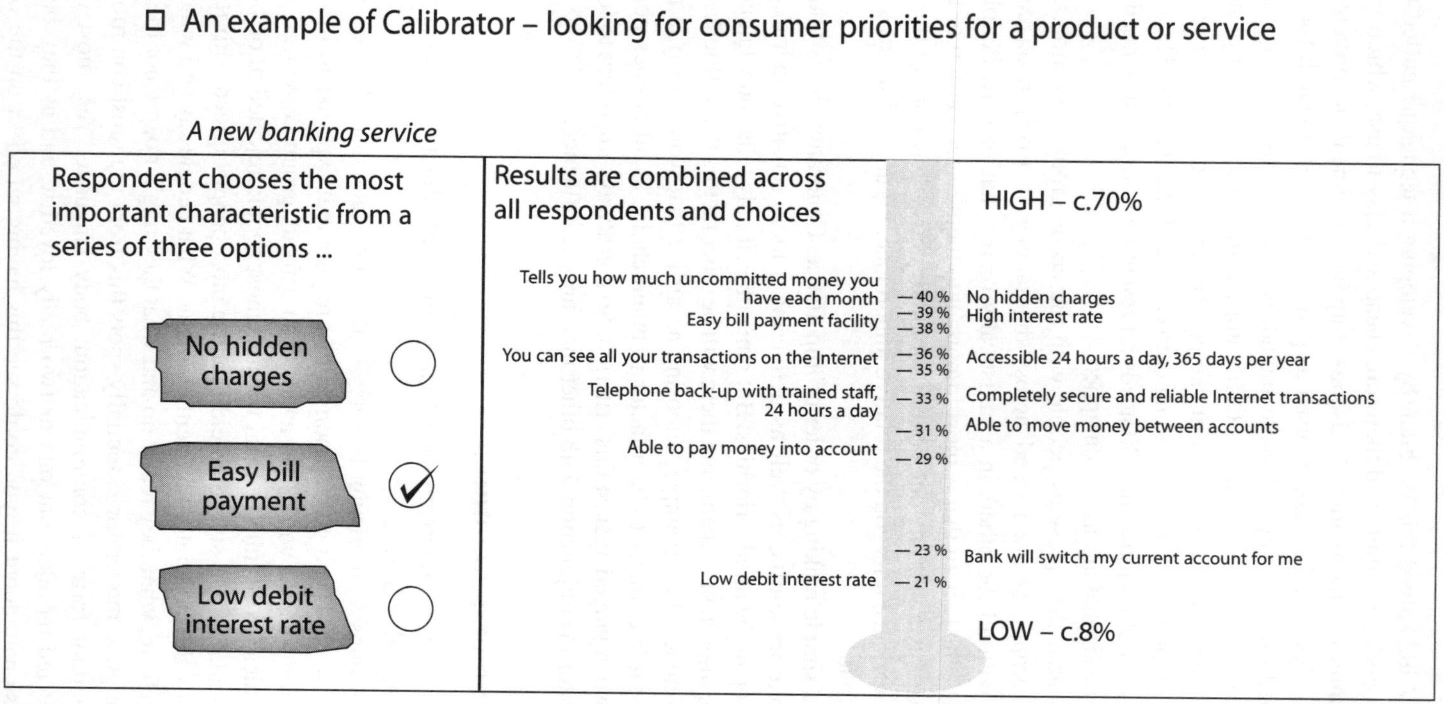

☐ An example of Calibrator – looking for consumer priorities for a product or service

A new banking service

Respondent chooses the most important characteristic from a series of three options ...

No hidden charges

Easy bill payment

Low debit interest rate

Results are combined across all respondents and choices

HIGH – c.70%

Tells you how much uncommitted money you have each month — 40 %   No hidden charges
Easy bill payment facility — 39 %   High interest rate
— 38 %
You can see all your transactions on the Internet — 36 %   Accessible 24 hours a day, 365 days per year
Telephone back-up with trained staff, 24 hours a day — 35 %   Completely secure and reliable Internet transactions
— 33 %   Able to move money between accounts
Able to pay money into account — 31 %
— 29 %
— 23 %   Bank will switch my current account for me
Low debit interest rate — 21 %

LOW – c.8%

Figure 1.5a Examples of Calibrator

The Calibrator for European grocery shopping

% of times mentioned store characteristic when asked

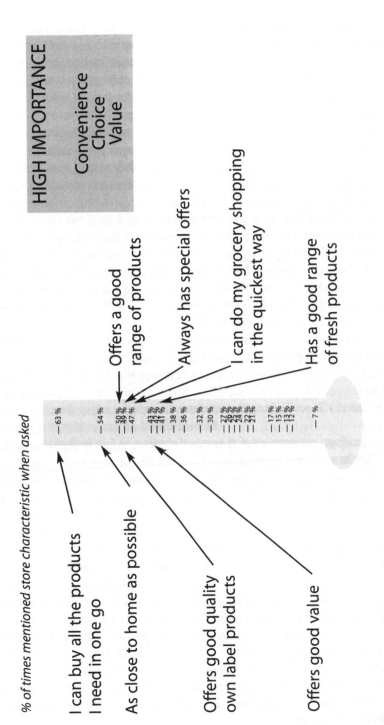

HIGH IMPORTANCE

Convenience
Choice
Value

I can buy all the products
I need in one go — 63 %

As close to home as possible — 54 %

Offers a good
range of products — 50 %, 47 %

Always has special offers — 43 %, 41 %

— 38 %
— 36 %

— 32 %
— 30 %

Offers good quality
own label products — 27 %, 26 %, 24 %, 22 %

I can do my grocery shopping
in the quickest way

Has a good range
of fresh products

— 17 %
— 15 %
— 13 %

Offers good value — 7 %

Figure 1.5b Examples of Calibrator

Yes, they mostly said they agreed with that point of view, but it wasn't consistent with what they said earlier and they said it with no real conviction.

When it comes to growth insights, people tend to like what they like, and find it hard to imagine how it could be improved. Moreover, they reject what they don't like and find it hard to be persuaded to reappraise because that makes them look foolish for having so strongly rejected it. So how do you cope with that? Good stimulus helps enormously, and it pays to put real thought, creativity and production costs into making it as good and varied as possible. Anything from simple word cards to rough visuals to beautifully produced videos can be employed. But you still have one tough problem to overcome. People are suspicious of researchers and marketers; they know they are being sold to and paid for their views, so they become simultaneously defensive and hypercritical. What is in truth a relatively unimportant purchase for them now requires them to act like a panel of fine wine tasters. The reality is often that they have no comment of value to make, but they'll find something to pick on, and because they don't want to lose face in front of others, they will defend their point of view. Or worse, they just switch off.

This is perhaps a little exaggerated. A good moderator is alert to this and has strategies to cope with the group effect, and the experience to interpret it and aim off. But if a European reader believes this is overly harsh, spare a thought for your American colleagues. Focus groups in the United States are mostly dire. The moderators are by and large low grade, and the stimulus mostly involves flash cards, 'Tell me what you think about this.' 'Well ma'am, I think it is just peachy.' 'Gee, that's swell, we're going to put it straight in a large survey and see whether a few thousand people agree with you.'

Is there any value in a consumer focus group? Absolutely, but the best results are obtained when they are used as a creative resource, as a way of producing ideas – what I call a 'consumer generator'. For a consumer generator, you need to recruit relatively articulate and creative people – simple recruitment questions can identify them. Then set up a three-hour session with lots of stimuli in the form of pictures, words, prototypes, raw materials, coloured pens, paper and glue. When they're ready, just dive the group into your category, your issues and your ideas – and watch. The output can be electric. There is always the concern that you have forced them to be enthusiastic and are therefore unable to judge their true passion for the ideas and the insights they come up with. But it is very easy to spot when they have come up with something because they were asked to, and when they have developed an idea that they are passionate about. And as you watch them work, they throw off insights the whole time in a much more natural and authentic way than in a focus group.

egg, a UK Internet bank, is the successful offshoot of the Prudential insurance company. Its success can really be attributed to the fact that it was effectively a first mover. There were some other Internet banks when it started out, but egg launched with more conviction and it felt like the first. The business was built from scratch with some of the team who had successfully developed First Direct, another successful banking offshoot, this time of HSBC (as it is now called). egg implemented a lot of the best practice that will be discussed in later sections – clear positioning in the market, strong values and sense of mission, the determination to build the competencies necessary for the new business away from the legacy business, fantastic products and services that were really differentiated. And they had this funny name. It wasn't so unusual in those crazy early days of dot.coms, and of course Apple had shown the way in computers, but it was very odd in mainstream financial services in the UK.

To help develop the precise set of services egg should have, its look and feel, and to get some reading on the name, we ran some consumer generators. We recruited groups of potential customers of this new bank, who were articulate and creative but otherwise fairly mainstream. They were not asked what they thought of the idea or the name, they were asked to develop it. For two and half hours they worked away designing this totally new bank which they were told was to be called egg. They were given some sample materials, mocked-up statements, a credit card, and lots of other materials to help them express their ideas. At no point until the end of the generator were they asked their opinion of the name – they were under the impression it had been decided. At the end of the generators we were able to get a true reading on the basic positioning for egg and its name, as well as many more insights on the precise services and how to present them. The people virtually fed back the intended strategy for the name. Yes, they said, at first it had sounded odd and they did not like it. But once they got used to it and more importantly were excited about the ideas they had developed for it, the name felt right. egg made them think of nest-eggs, things that grow, a fresh start, and the idea that although eggs look the same they turn into something very individual. In fact, a bank that treats you like an individual was the key idea that the team had developed for egg.

Those consumer generators delivered more insights than just the confirmation of the name, but the confidence they produced about egg as a name illustrates the power of this insight technique. Conventional research would almost certainly have provided the ammunition for the doubters, not just in Prudential but in our own team, to reject egg for something a little safer. I was not an official member of the team, but when asked for my advice I said I hated egg. I am now a very happy customer.

5. Segmentation or market mapping

All progress in marketing is based on market segmentation, and sometimes, but not always, this involves redefining the market. Along with benefit trade-offs and brand positioning, segmentation is the essential tool of the marketer. Artists have their palette and paints, musicians their instruments, the soldier his gun. The marketer has segmentation with which to paint new pictures, create new melodies and kill the enemy. It's just that segmentation doesn't sound very sexy. So we renamed it market mapping which not only sounds a little sexier – think of Marco Polo or Columbus, exploring the world, challenging conventional thinking, creating new charts and maps, opening up new trading possibilities – it also sounds more useful. Maps tell you where you are and where you can go. Different maps can show different pictures of the world, not just its geographic boundaries but also climate, agriculture, ideologies and how they all relate. Marketers must be more than alchemists; they must be explorers, adventurers, scientists and cartologists.

Segmentation or market mapping is the art and science of cutting a market into different groupings that explain choice. There is a kind of history of segmentation that provides a commentary of how marketing has developed. To begin with, manufacturers segmented markets by type of product. For example:

- Draught beers or packaged beers
- Countlines or weight bars in confectionery (a Mars bar or bar of choco-late to you and me)
- High speed and low speed photocopiers
- Saloon cars or sports cars
- Mainframe computers or personal computers.

This was the early days of marketing, when the predominant philosophy was to sell what you make. Then the marketers started to assert themselves: 'We should make what we sell, and that means we must think from the customer's point of view.' Businesses started to segment not by product type but by type of consumer or customer:

- Small, medium and large enterprises
- Men or women
- Extroverts or introverts
- Health nuts or indulgers
- Left-handed or right-handed people.

The first four examples seem obvious for industries such as professional services, personal products, fashion and food respectively, but left-handed and right-handed? It is actually quite important if you make scissors, golf clubs and certain musical instruments. The fact is, different groups of people have different needs, attitudes and priorities. Understand this, and we understand how we can offer different choices.

This form of consumer segmentation reached its peak in the late 1990s, with consumer values segmentation. The world is divided into two types of consultant, the type who think there are two kinds of people and the kind who don't. The former actually believe there are roughly six types of people who can be grouped according to their values, something akin to Maslow's hierarchy of needs with a bit of introvert and extrovert thrown in. All brand choice can be explained by understanding which group you fall into. Er … no, it can't, actually. People fall into different groupings, depending on the category in question. The person who is confident and outgoing when it comes to choosing a car may be unconfident and introvert when it comes to choosing a pension or mortgage. So brand choice needs to take into account other factors.

Those other factors were initially captured in the odd expression 'needstates' (when was the last time you went to the doctor with a painstate?). A small row broke out in marketing circles about who first came up with needstates, but Wendy Gordon probably has the best claim. Her idea was built on the other emerging type of segmentation, needs segmentation. This is the idea that markets could be explained by looking at different groupings of needs:

- To be pretty or healthy
- To be indulged or energised
- To feel like an individual or to feel part of a group
- To go fast or to be safe
- To be refreshed or to be comforted.

The final way of segmenting the market relates to the distribution channel, which is a widely used form of market segmentation, but more common in sales and operations than in marketing. It's often used in isolation from other factors, but would cover, for example:

- Branch or telephone or Internet or sales force or intermediaries
- On-trade or off-trade
- Grocery or impulse trade
- Retail or mail order
- Owned or franchised.

So there are many ways of segmenting a market and many maps you can draw.

There need now be no argument between the various schools of thought on segmentation. We can look at the market through any of their windows. The trick is to combine them in the most effective and appropriate way.

Listening to a comedy sketch on the radio one night, I heard a hilarious spoof of the trainee journalist trying to file a story but getting in a complete muddle over the who, when, what, why, where that journalists are taught to use. A large penny dropped. These are exactly the headings by which you can segment or map a market: the Five W's (see Figure 1.6).

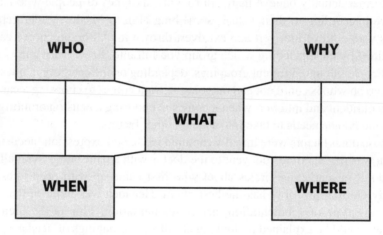

Figure 1.6 The Five 'W's

Each of the Five Ws in part explains how choices are made in the market, but the whole picture emerges when they are seen in relation to each other. Some people buy these products for these needs or benefits on these occasions from these places. You can cut in at any of the W's, but let's start in the middle with 'What?'

What?	This relates to the first stage of our history of segmentation – segmenting the market by type of product.
Who?	The marketer's favourite, and the second stage in our history – segmenting by type of customer.
Why?	Segment the market by 'needstates' – the different motivations to buy and benefits offered.
When?	Not covered in the history of segmentation above, the When? approach looks at segmenting according to the occasions when people buy a product.
Where?	Segmenting the market by distribution channel.

But enough of the theory of segmentation. Let's move on to an example that will illustrate the opening premise – that all progress depends on cutting the market a different way to offer different solutions. Here are a few ways of segmenting the drinks market. Notice that each segment cuts the market, the Five W's, a different way to offer a different solution.

- If we can only offer the planet one drink it has to be water. (It does, after all, cover most of the earth's surface.)
- Tired people in search of stimulation and a little comforting, when taking a break from work, drink coffee, which they buy in Starbucks or from a vending machine or make themselves.
- Blokes (lads, mates, 'the boys'), after mid-week soccer training, all drink draught lager, in their neighbourhood pub, for refreshment and comradeship. The same guy, taking his girl out on a Friday night (or on the pull), drinks a fancy import beer from the bottle, in a club or bar, to look cool.
- Health-conscious people, at home in the morning, in search of healthy and nutritional refreshment, drink orange juice, which they probably bought in the supermarket.
- After sport you need to hydrate and replace minerals in a way the body can most easily absorb, and you are in a hurry, so you buy an isotonic drink from a vending machine.

We are going to return to market mapping and the Five W's because as may already be apparent, having the right market map and the right ideas about how to rewrite it lies at the heart of not just insight but also ideas, innovation, impact and investment return. It is a fundamental strategic tool that drives overall strategy as well as portfolio and brand strategy. It can answer questions like, how do you define your market? Where do you want to compete? And with what competitive advantage? Market mapping is the basis of new innovation, creating new categories in which you can be first, planning your communications and marketplace impact, and measuring the returns according to the segments you were targeting.

So how do you create a market map? The first step is to gather together all the internal information you have – existing research, the experience held in the heads of people who really know your business and market, your agencies, published reports and whatever else you can get your hands on. Then get a small but select group into a workshop for a day, and start by agreeing a market definition. Use all the insights you have gathered at the first stage as stimulus for the workshop.

If you were creating a market map for a pain relief brand, a simple exercise would be to ask participants why and when they would take a pain relief tablet. As you write their answers on a flip chart, you should quickly see more reasons than the expected answer, 'Because I had a headache.' They could include, 'Because I had a hangover', 'I had a terrible cold', 'Because I dropped a dumbbell on my foot', and so on. A next step is to take each of these occasions and ask people to write up everything they could use on that occasion that would satisfy their need. This in itself normally offers some insights, as the brand team would start to see that although they are in the pain relief market, they actually compete against a wide variety of other products: a glass of water (people often get headaches when dehydrated), Lemsip (traditional cold relief) and even McDonald's (a commonly referenced hangover cure!).

This would give you an extremely broad view of your market, and it is important to rein this in. Determining the right market definition is an important output from this stage of the process, and to do this you need to consider some key factors:

- the trade-off between the depth of information and the new opportunities you get from the breadth of coverage
- the kind of growth opportunities you are looking for (short, medium or long-term solution)
- your business capabilities
- your competitive ambition.

Next, work through each of the Five W's and without agonising too much, just list the headings of people, needs or benefits, product types, occasions, places of distribution or usage. The lists should not be too long – there should be a maximum of eight items under each W, although five is probably better. It is very important that you do not try to establish any linkages between the various W's until you have listed and agreed them all.

When you've done all that, draw some big circles and group together, roughly, the clusters of W's. A different W can often dominate a different circle. For example in salty snacks there is one dominant circle, which is about the 'why' (gap fill), but another that is more about a 'who', kids (small treat).

The size of the circle should roughly approximate to the size of the segment. Put the biggest in the middle, since it normally corresponds to what this market is really all about. If we did this for all drinks we would have social refreshment in the middle. That is your first draft map, and it is normally at least 60 per cent accurate, so you can go on to place the brands in the market on the map and start to look at why they might over-index or under-index in any one segment or for any one grouping under each of the W's. Insights will already start to flow.

Let's look at a few different markets and think about the kind of insights

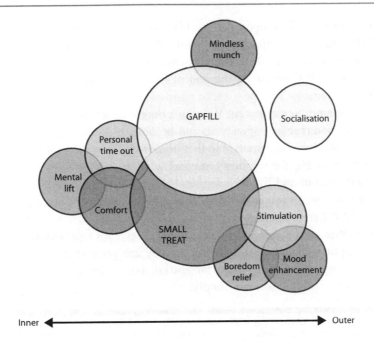

Figure 1.7 Market mapping for salty snacks

Source: Added Value Need States Study (UK)

this technique could have produced. (I'm not saying that market mapping was used in all these cases – but it certainly would come as no surprise if it had been.)

- There are no relatively healthy soft drinks that kids like – so let's create Sunny Delight.
- Watches are fashion accessories and young people would like to own more than one – so let's produce Swatches.
- Personal computers make no statement about you, they are ugly – so let's design the iMac.
- Ice creams don't represent the same degree of indulgence as chocolate confectionery – so let's bring out Magnum.
- Some people want retro cars with modern usability rather than the cost and unreliability of a second-hand classic – so how about building the Beetle, the Mazda MX5, the PT cruiser?

Once you've produced the market map, you need to verify it. Run some consumer generators based on your hypotheses. Give the people all the headings you have developed for the Five W's, but in everyday language, plus all the brands you think are in this market, and make sure they can add things you may have missed. Then essentially put them through the same exercise you went through. At the end of this your map is probably 70–80 per cent accurate.

Next do quantitative research. Without going into too much of the technical detail, a good research agency should be able to do the analysis that will give you a statistically accurate map that demonstrates with reasonable precision exactly how big the segments are and what are the key determinants of choice, both overall and for each segment. If you have included some trade-off questions, it will show how different segments trade off different benefits according to different occasions.

Having done all this, reconvene your workshop team and review the findings, but capture all the fresh insights as they are presented. Some will be blindingly simple and some more tangential, but make sure that everyone realises exactly what **action** they imply.

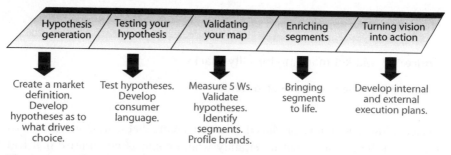

Figure 1.8 The Five 'W's process

I have now conducted so many of these exercises that some general patterns emerge. In low unit price, high frequency purchase markets like snacks and drinks, the occasion, and the need that relates to it, is the dominant driver. Statistically there is more difference between the brand choice made on different occasions than there is between brand choices made by two different types of people. Or put another way, on certain occasions we all choose the fancy import beer and on other occasions we all choose the standard beer.

Cars are the opposite: we do not buy a repertoire of cars to drive on different occasions according to the occasion or the person we want to be (or at least not unless we are very rich, in which case that is exactly what we do). But ordinary folk buy just the one car, and that is fundamentally a reflection of their socio-demographics (single/poor or married with kids/well off, or more often the other way around) and their values (conservative, extrovert, individual).

If you want proof of the value of this exercise, just take 30 minutes to work through it for cinema films. If you need a kick start, go down to your local video shop. They will have done some of the work for you, since the videos are grouped under certain headings. Watch who is renting what, and if you feel brave ask them a few questions about why they have made their choice, what they think is important in a film, and who will be watching it with them.

What	Who	Why	When	Where
Action (e.g. *Gladiator*)	Gang of teens	Escapism	Weekend social	Local cinema
Drama (e.g. *Remains of of the Day*)	Young couples	Stimulation	Mid-week – something to do	Inner city entertainment centre
	Older couples	Relaxation	Date	
Horror (e.g. *Friday the Thirteenth*)	Family with kids	Boredom/ passing time	First date	Plane
				Hotel
Sci-Fi (e.g. *The Matrix*)	Traveller	Education/ curiosity	Specific occasion	Home
Comedy (e.g. *Four Weddings*)		Social bonding	Holiday treat	Drive-in
Romance (e.g. *Sleepless in Seattle*)			Bored and lonely (time fillers)	
Cartoon (e.g. *Shrek*)				
Young adventure (e.g. *Star Wars*)				
Young comedy (e.g. *Nutty Professor*)				

Figure 1.9 The Five 'W's and the movies

Your map will look roughly like Figure 1.11 (overleaf). For simplicity, this chart has been based on 'whys' but it could be based on any of the other Five 'W's.

Here are a few insights that might be revealed:

Films compete in a wider market that include eating out and video games.
We could make films more interactive and bundle them with food offerings. Home delivery pizza companies could add top movies to their menus (a few do apparently).

Schindler's List is hard to place in any segment yet it was a very popular film.

Segments	Entertain us	Young thrills	Sit back and enjoy	Kill time	Shared pleasure	Talking point
Why	Escapism	Stimulation	Relaxation	Boredom/ passing time	Social bonding	Education/ curiosity
What	Drama Action Young comedy	Horror Sci-Fi Comedy Young adventure	Drama Romance comedy	Any	Action Drama Comedy Young adventure Young comedy	Sci-Fi Horror Young adventure
Who	All	Gang of teens Young couples (Family with kids)	Older couples Young couples	Traveller Older couples	Gang of teens Family with kids	Gang of teens Young couples Family with kids
When	Weekend social Date/first date	Weekend social Special occasion Holiday treat First date	Weekend social Mid-week (something to do) Bored and lonely Date/first date	Mid-week (something to do) Bored and lonely	Special occasion Holiday treat	Any
Where	Any	Inner city entertainment centre Drive-in	Local cinema Home Drive-in	Home Plane Hotel	Inner city entertainment centre	Local cinema Inner city entertainment centre Home

Notes:

1. The matrix, which will form the basis of the map, has been oriented to the 'why'. It could have been any of the 'W's.
2. The 'W's indicated show the sub-segments that over-index to that particular 'W'.
3. Quantitative research would give the statistical clusters. A cluster could be dominated by any of the 'W's: an occasion, a type of cinema-goer, a type of film or place.
4. The names given to the clusters are meant to be simple aides-memoire. We could have named them A, B, C, D, E and F.

Figure 1.10 Movie market segments

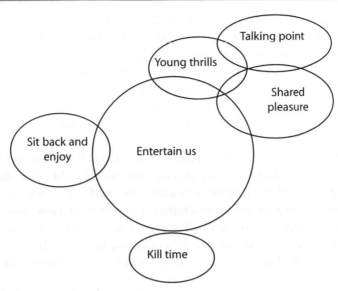

Figure 1.11 Market mapping for movies

This is because it is a cathartic experience similar to Greek tragedies. Is this a potentially new segment appealing to particular people on certain occasions?

There are brands of films linked to an actor, director, producer or company (such as an Arnie movie or a Disney movie) that offer consistent benefits to the audience and compete in clear segments of the market.
Other actors, producers or companies deliberately avoid being so stereotyped, and for the most part they make less money. This is because stars act as brands for film audiences, guaranteeing a certain kind of movie experience: for example, Bruce Willis means action, while Hugh Grant means romantic comedy. When Disney wanted to enter the teen/action market, it needed to create a new brand, because it was too clearly identified with the kids market.

Education is a big market and films are a big market, but the segment for educational films is small and there is no 'brand'.
Are there opportunities here that media and education giants like the BBC or Pearson should be looking to exploit?

Films watched at home and films watched in the cinema offer two different experiences.
Cinemas offer better quality viewing, a group experience, an event, and the chance to be the first to see it. Renting at home is more accessible, flexible, and you can watch films you might be too embarrassed to go to the cinema

to see, or might feel are not worth the investment of time and money. But home viewing is getting closer to cinema. There is a new 'who' and 'when' emerging, as people invest in high quality in-home entertainment, and create occasions when they order in pizzas, invite their friends and make more of an event of it. What more could be done to close the gap? How do cinemas make it more of an experience? Or should they go the other way and offer a Starbucks version – of small outlets – or one-hour versions of films?

That last question is an interesting one. 'If Starbucks opened a chain of cinemas and/or started making movies, how would it do it?' It shows how thinking can be challenged by contrasting one market map with another map in an adjacent area, or indeed in a totally different field. How would another major brand enter your market and apply its map and its patterns and preconceptions? How would it target the occasions, benefits, channels and people for which it has become famous and for which it has developed the competencies? For example:

- Why is there no super-premium offer in films like there is in luxury goods or cars? How would Versace present films or Ferrari do home entertainment?
- Is Disney the Sunny Delight or Captain Birds Eye of films – both brands smuggle a bit of goodness into kids – or could this edutainment be done better?

The answers to such questions should generate real insight and lead to a rich vein of inspiration and innovation.

HOW TO SPOT THE EUREKA MOMENT

This chapter has suggested a few places to look for insight and examined a few techniques for tracking it down. We have searched for those insights that will inspire the idea or strategy that will lead to change, innovation and ultimately solid gold top-line growth for your business. But how do you evaluate the output of this process? How do you know when you have found your Philosopher's Stone?

First, you need to ensure that you understand the significance of the insights you have gathered. So for every piece of insight work, capture the output in a succinct form. Not a waffly report but a crisp set of bullet points or a paragraph. By all means, where appropriate, bring this alive, but make sure it is crystal clear.

Next assemble the team and choose a venue – and do both with great care. The wrong team in some windowless meeting room will not produce alchemy. The team should be motivated, diverse, committed to growth, experts with open minds. Don't choose by rank, choose by talent – there will be time for the politics later. The venue should be off-site, special, big, airy and mind-expanding.

You need to enter the session with a mission for growth. You need something you are looking for, some sense of where you are and where you would like to be – and this must be spelt out and agreed with the group.

Don't worry if you find yourself selecting a different destination from the one you had intended: remember Christopher Columbus. He set out to find a new route to the East Indies and its fabled riches. But when he struck land in the Caribbean, far from being discouraged, he resourcefully concluded that he'd found the 'West' Indies and, having misnamed the indigenous people 'Indians', returned to claim his place in history. Of course Columbus had been nowhere near his intended destination, but had he not had a mission he would never have set sail, nor would he have known how to run a ship or manage a crew. And he would certainly never have made his mark had he not been prepared to re-evaluate what he found.

Then let the alchemical processes begin. Review the insights, present them, challenge them, build on them and allow them to collide. Every success story you have ever admired used this technique, although it may have happened in a partial or haphazard way. The whole process may even have occurred intuitively in the head of an individual entrepreneur. All that is being offered here is a more reliable method based on experience.

How will you know the insight is a great one? You won't for sure (at least until you see the sales figures) but you can always ask these five simple questions:

- Is it fresh? Do you feel you are looking at your market and your mission in a new way, even if the insight is really simple?
- Is it discerning? Do you feel you can compare it with other viable alternatives and confidently say it is better?
- Is it penetrating? Does it get beyond superficial analysis and conventional wisdom? Do you feel you have gone deeper into the market than anyone else before you?
- Is it the product or the fusion of more than one insight, or if you have chosen one simple insight, can you see how it links to other insights?
- Does it inspire you and others? Are the implications already starting to flow for how you can change strategy, innovate, communicate in new ways, see different things you will now measure for success?

If you can honestly answer yes to all of these, you have a great insight – maybe not the greatest – but great enough to build the idea.

The Levi's Engineered Jeans case study, which is in Appendix 2, was written for a market research audience, so it focuses on the market analysis and research techniques used, but it does not expose the true alchemy that went on. In addition to the insights the team gathered from history, the market, adjacent markets, the opinion leaders, the experts, the semiotics and the market mapping, there were two other key factors. The first was the fact that Levi's had developed excellent partnerships with the suppliers of denim, and they were inputting stimulating new insights about denim from a technical point of view. The second was the Levi's design team, who were both creative and really knowledgeable about the market. In fact they themselves were great alchemists who needed only the stimulation of other insights to be able to conceive engineered jeans. There was one seminal moment in the process when a young fashion designer, part of the expert panel, said, 'It's like they (Levi's 501's) are trying to hold the fabric back from what it was originally intended to do.'

In hindsight this was felt by the team to be a critical insight, but I believe it was a match that ignited all the insights into the one vision that became Levi's Engineered Jeans. Research subsequently honed and directed the idea, and Levi's implemented it well, but the alchemy had already occurred. Everyone knew that they had heard a fresh, discerning, penetrating fusion of insights – and that is what ignited their inspiration.

THE STUFF THAT GETS IN THE WAY OF INSIGHT

1. No clarity of purpose

Insights for growth come when people in the business are clear that they are looking for growth – as opposed to cost savings, implementation, or just keeping the 'system' happy.

2. Too few insightful people in the wrong jobs

Anyone can be coached to be more insightful and alert to insights, but undoubtedly some are better at it than others. It is rarely the case that a truly insightful person is also a good implementer, and yet people are normally expected to be both, or worse, the insightful are stuck in implementation jobs. It is not difficult to spot the people who are genuinely insightful; the trick is to give them the stimulus and the freedom to perform the insight alchemy, and then to put them in teams where others can take the insights forward.

3. No mechanism to capture the insights

Insights come from a variety of sources both inside and outside the business, but there is often no forum outside a project team for those insights to come together. Entrepreneurial leaders have insights because a) they have the freedom to roam around and make connections and b) they never have to make an appointment with themselves. The normal company strategic planning process or annual brand plans do not provide a forum or a process for all the potential sources of insight to be shared and allowed to ignite – in the context of a strategic purpose, of course.

4. The consumer is not king

If the process was as simple as asking people, forming strategy from the findings, giving the brief to the technical folk and bringing it to market, we'd all be heroes. The consumer part of the equation is overdone, and as noted above, there are too few mechanisms to allow the consumer insight to spark off all the other insights.

5. Insights are not written down

Insights, like ideas, often seem to coalesce in businesses, but nobody ever writes them down in plain simple English. But if you do this, you open up the possibility for people to challenge or maybe even build on the insight. And if and when things go wrong it allows you to retrace your steps – was it the insight that was wrong or what we did with it? Like many people, I am heartily fed up with case studies that rewrite history. 'Our reading of the market was that ...' It would be so much more convincing simply to identify the time the key insight occurred, and to produce the piece of paper on which someone wrote it down.

Ideas

IDEAS AND STRATEGY

Some senior people in organisations are wary of the word 'ideas'. As far as
they're concerned, ideas are for hairy people with odd socks who never use
the percentage key on their calculators. Instead of 'kicking ideas around',
boardroom types like to 'talk strategy'. Indeed, at the very mention of the
word 'strategy', brows furrow and consultants rub their hands. 'Strategy' is
a serious and expensive business – whereas 'having ideas' sounds like too
much fun. Certainly, if you're ever writing a brief for a consultant, the use
of the word 'strategic' will instantly add a 100 per cent premium to the price.
But try asking for a few ideas and you should be pleasantly surprised by the
quote you receive.

Unfortunately, most people – including very senior people – do not know what 'strategy' actually means. I have proved this many times at the beginning of a strategy workshop by asking for a few definitions of the word. The responses normally include some reference to one or all of the following – a plan, an objective, something for the long term. They are all partly right but they all miss the point of strategy. In a recent forum of senior business heads in a major consumer goods business, the CEO put up a slide that stated the strategy was 'high double digit growth'. He was perplexed when one of his senior team pointed out that this was a goal, and asked if they were to be told how they were going to achieve this. So, what do we mean by 'strategy'?

To settle the debate, let's look it up in the *Oxford English Dictionary*. The definition it gives is very illuminating:

The art of war... the art of so moving or disposing troops or ships or aircraft as to impose upon the enemy the place and time and conditions for fighting preferred by oneself.

It goes on to say that strategy can also refer to the plan that captures this art. Even more interestingly, it refers you to 'tactics', where exactly the same definition is given, with the addition of the words 'in actual contact with the enemy'. In other words, 'tactics' is strategy plus action. So if you issue a tactical brief you get the strategy – a few insightful ideas – and some indication of how to put it into practice, all for less than you would have paid for a full-blown 'strategy review'.

But despite the CEO's embarrassment over confusing a strategy and a goal, there was some truth in what he had said. In business, strategy is certainly about growth. In fact, there is no other kind of strategy. And in terms of the Five 'I's process, a strategy is simply an idea driven by an insight – or better still, driven by an inspirational combination of them. Nobody ever implemented a long strategic document; people implement ideas. And any idea for growth relies on the quality of the insights gained at the first stage of the Five 'I's process. Successful implementation then requires creativity – that is to say, fresh connections – and some kind of sacrifice. Here's an example to illustrate the point.

In the battle of Agincourt (historians please don't get too picky), the English knew that their knights on horseback, the elite of the army, were no match for their French counterparts. But it had been raining, so the battlefield was very muddy, which meant that heavily armoured knights would struggle anyway – and the English were more confident in their archers. The normal rules of engagement were for the knights to slug it out first, then the archers would fire off their arrows at each other, and finally the foot soldiers together with the knights that were left would slug it out all over again. The French duly sent their knights onto the field of battle. They looked fantastic as only French knights could do, but they looked less fantastic as they slowly sank into the mud. The English knights held back and instead let their archers pick off the French knights from a safe distance. Then they sent in the soldiers and knights on horseback and a great victory was won – basically, because they cheated. Or to put it another way, they used insight, analysis and some creative thinking to challenge the rules and achieve an unlikely win over a seemingly superior enemy.

Despite all the patriotic windbagging that Agincourt has produced over the centuries, the English victory can still be used to demonstrate five of the crucial aspects of strategy that are highlighted in the OED definition:

- **You need an enemy.** The French army, the market leader, the irritating start-up down the road; take your pick.
- **It is about winning.** And in both business and war, what constitutes a win is clear. It's victory and conquest. It's top line growth and market domination. To put it another way, it's about defining your Key Performance Indicators and making sure you achieve them.
- **It is based on a combination of insights** ... into weather conditions, market conditions, relative strengths and weaknesses, rules of engagement, market conventions...The list, as we've seen, is endless.
- **It is about assets and how to deploy them.** Knights, brands, archers, adverts, foot soldiers, sales reps – you draw the parallels.
- **It requires you to change the rules.** It doesn't matter whether you challenge expectations in the salty snacks market or the received wisdom in infantry tactics, the key thing is to challenge and change the way things get done.

There are legions of books on business strategy, many of which draw the parallel with war, although fewer highlight the importance of insight and ideas. In one of the best books available, *Competing for the Future,*[1] Hammel and Prahalad make the point that strategy is 'stretch' – it emerges from the gap between your goals and your resources. In another excellent book, *Built to Last: Successful Habits of Visionary Companies,* Collins and Porras[2] talk about the importance of a BHAG or 'big hairy audacious goal', but one set in the context of a) some overall sense of purpose – a cause noble enough to inspire generations of managers – and b) a sense of values – the way you conduct business.

These two fine books, which complement each other very well, go into a lot of detail and provide many examples of successful business strategy. *Competing for the Future,* in particular, offers some very good strategic tools and frameworks that are an improvement on the mainstay of strategic analysis, the SWOT analysis (strengths, weaknesses, opportunities and threats). Hammel and Prahalad emphasise not just their idea of 'stretch', but also the importance of being clear about the competencies you have and the competencies you will need to compete in future markets. The quality of their insights is highlighted by the work that Gary Hammel has gone on to do for companies such as Nokia in Finland. His insights certainly helped to shape Nokia's strategic idea that mobile phones were about far more than mobile communication. Their use as status symbols, worry beads and even instruments of social grooming, especially among young people, owes much to Hammel's emphasis on this type of insight.

But however inspired and sophisticated the work on business strategy has been, much of it boils down to answering five very simple questions:

1. What is our purpose – or mission? To put it another way, what is the mark we want to leave on the world?
2. What is our market?
3. Who are our competitors?
4. Who are our buyers?
5. What are we good at and how does this stack up against the success factors in our market?

You need to be able to answer these questions with insight – and questions 2 to 5 need to be answered for both the present and the future. But if, after a great deal of thought, you can write down those answers on one piece of paper, you have the basis of an idea for growth, otherwise known as a strategy. Here are three examples of companies which had ideas for growth and knew how to implement them.

Nike had a sense of mission. Started by athletes, it wanted to be the number one sports brand in the world – an outrageous idea, when it first conceived it. It redefined the market from running shoes to all sports equipment, and redefined its competitors in the process. It identified new buyers beyond just athletes. It combined technical design skills with fashion design skills, and built superior branding and sourcing competencies. It changed the rules and the way we think about both sport and sports gear.

Diageo is another company that knows the value of challenging and changing the rules. At one time, the drinks market was all about spirits, wine and beer. Down the pub, this translated into pints and shorts. But Diageo realised that it needn't be like this. A long drink didn't have to mean a lager or a bitter. It focused on the idea of a long, adult, social, refreshing drink and created Smirnoff Ice – a long spirits-based drink in a bottle which had particular appeal to women socialising in pubs and bars.

For a long time, Marks and Spencer was a company famous for the clarity of its strategic ideas: the promises of quality and value for money were obvious from the moment you stepped into one of its shops. But by the end of the 1990s, it had become apparent that the company had lost its way and allowed other retailers like Next and Gap to move onto its natural territory. It was only by rediscovering the meaning of its original strategic idea that Marks and Spencer was able to fight back and find its way out of the woods.

In truth, all these case studies work better with hindsight, and great execution probably played a bigger part than brilliant conception. But whether or not the examples follow the strict letter of the theory, in all cases the companies had an insight into some or all aspects of their business: the market, human nature, history, the competition and themselves. And they turned those insights into a successful strategic idea.

As the Marks and Spencer example shows, successful strategic ideas can be born of the fear of failure – but the problem is that the fear ends after the first flush of success. Sustained growth has to be built on an emotion that is not so easily fulfilled – what is fashionably called 'passion'. Genuine passion – for a stretch goal, for a BHAG, or even for solid gold top-line growth – is something that never ends. And passion is the oxygen of true strategic ideas and growth.

At Added Value, we worked on the development of the Guinness Brewing Global Strategy in the mid-1990s with the board of the company. A perfectly logical and robust strategic plan was in place, but the board were concerned that it was almost too logical and too neat. They wanted to challenge themselves, to see if they had missed other sources for growth, possibly outside their core business. We conducted a series of one-on-one stakeholder interviews to get all the issues out on the table. What were the hunches? What did they think they were really good at and could leverage? What were they bad at and needed to improve? At the offsite workshop this was presented back, and it culminated in a deliberately over-intellectual chart, indicating the possible future sources of growth, typical of the kind of analysis a management consultant would use (see Figure 2.2).

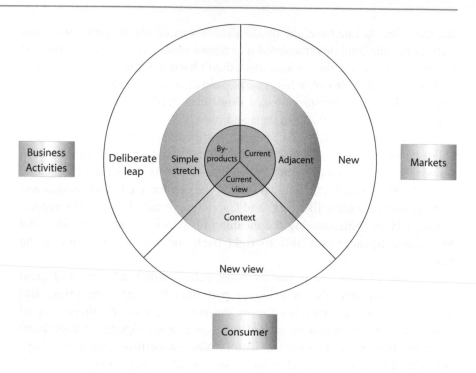

Figure 2.2 New growth: the intellectual approach

It was discussed for a few minutes with no real conclusion and frankly, not a lot of passion either. After a theatrical pause the next chart was put up. It said very simply:

> ## What would you kill to do?
> ## What might kill you if you don't do it?

Of course we knew the answer from the preparation work. Although they rarely admitted it to themselves, the board really loved Guinness, the drink. They were more than just managers, in their hearts they were disciples, custodians of, in their opinion, one of the greatest brands and the greatest beer in the world. The answer came back clearly and with passion, 'We have to grow Guinness, but more than that, it's what we really want to do.' That became the rallying call in the company, the start of a whole new strategy and a new set of tactics that regenerated growth in the business.

But even great insights and true passion do not guarantee that strategic ideas will translate into top-line growth. You can never test strategy, you can only ever test the assumptions on which it's based – and it is always a good idea to do so. A strategic idea should be chosen from a range of options, and at least part of that choice should be informed by analysis, even if the final choice is based on passion. But by itself a great strategic idea is still not enough; the critical tests will come in its execution, when its success will depend on external factors and the flexibility with which you react to them.

As Christopher Columbus showed, there needs to be enough breadth and flex in your ideas to permit changes in emphasis. You need to be able to see what is working and to increase the effort behind it, and to ditch what is not working. Collins and Porras, in their analysis of successful long term businesses, point to the number of times that great businesses had less than successful beginnings. Even Sony found that its initial products failed, but there was enough passion and enough flexibility in the company to regroup, make changes and press on.

Once Sir Bobby Robson, the former England football coach, was getting frustrated in a press conference when he was being criticized for the lack of fluency in his team's play. 'Look,' he said, 'if you want fluent play, come and watch us practise. The problem is, when we get out on the pitch, there are 11 other men who are trying to stop us doing that.'

HOW TO 'DO IT DIFFERENT'

Michael Porter, undoubtedly one of the great gurus of strategic ideas, says that there are essentially two growth strategies: 'do it better or do it different'. Both are valid, but in the rest of this chapter, we'll share his macho disregard for the adverb and focus on 'doing it different'. To be more specific we are going to cover the following:

1. Defining the market.
2. Market mapping.
3. Brand portfolios.
4. Brand positioning.
5. Brand extension and architecture.

We will then conclude with a summary of winning strategies or ideas.

1. Defining the market

How you define your market, in relation to your overall mission, is the critical first step. There comes a point in the history of every successful company when it needs to be able to look at its market with fresh eyes and gain a genuinely new insight into its relationship with it. It is often too comfortable for companies to jog along selling the same kind of thing, making the occasional tweak perhaps, but never really re-evaluating their market. These companies have become fixated on "What?' In other words, they are only asking themselves the question, 'What are we selling?' To realise their true growth potential, they need to start asking "Why?' and start understanding the real reason for their market's existence. Here are a few examples of companies which have done just that:

- Mars bars used to define its market as countline confectionery bars. Judging by its actions it now defines it as all chocolate indulgence, since it markets ice cream, a drink, mini Mars bars, mini Mars ice cream for sharing and so on.
- Tesco used to define its market as grocery retailing. It now sells petrol, household goods, financial services, clothes, books and many more items to do with running the household.
- Dove used to see its market as toilet soap bars. It now has a range that includes moisturiser, shampoo, deodorant and shower wash, which addresses a much bigger market of personal products to do with improving women's skin.
- Car companies recognised that their market was not just cars but anything relating to the acquisition and running of a car, including financial services.
- Virgin, who have expanded fairly opportunistically, address markets where there is a role for a 'consumer champion' to fight the fat cats and change the rules.

In many cases the idea for a new range and the redefinition of the market would have come simultaneously, and there is certainly room for opportunism and serendipity in defining market. But it is still a really good discipline to write down, in plain English, a definition of your market in terms of both the 'Why?' and the 'What?' This will in itself often reveal a growth insight that leads to an important strategic idea.

2. Market mapping

Market mapping has already been covered in the chapter on Insight. But understanding how your market currently segments along the five dimensions – who? what? why? when? where? – and how these relate to each other, is not just a source of insight, but also the prime source of a strategic ideas.

Every successful strategic idea resegments the market, redraws the map and changes the rules of engagement so that you fight the battle on your own terms. Whether inspired by people, other markets or technical insights, a strategic idea can be based on introducing new benefits or redefining existing ones (new 'Whys?') new occasions (new 'Whens?'), new channels (new 'Wheres?'), appealing to a new group of people, (new 'Whos?') and/or making new connections between all of these. Think of Tango, originally a kiddy fruit carbonate which was connected to a new 'Who?' – an older teen audience with attitude. Or what about four wheel drives, which started life as utility vehicles for the countryside and ended up as high status cars offering improved vision and safety for city drivers, especially women with families?

So how is market mapping used to generate strategic ideas? Well, assuming you are already in the market, the first thing to analyse is where you currently compete. If you have done a quantified market map you should have the data for this, but even a quick judgmental look can be revealing. With the benefit of no data at all, let's look at Coke, who apparently want to compete everywhere (see Figure 2.3). What we are looking for is where Coke under-indexes or over-indexes in any one part of the map compared to its overall market share. Or to put it more simply – where are its strengths and weaknesses? To bring into play the idea of market definition, we'll look at the overall beverage market, but it's worth noting that the fact Coke competes with tea, coffee and alcohol is, in itself, a strategic idea. However, this also explains why Coke scores well on stimulation versus other soft drinks, but under-performs and therefore under-indexes versus beverages overall.

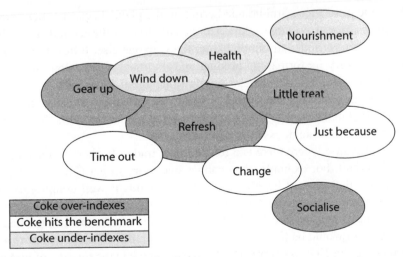

Figure 2.3 Market mapping for Coke

The conclusions we draw from this are the starting point of a strategic idea for growth. The success of Coke lies in its ability to compete in large chunks of the map, but there are clear choices of where it can go, based on this simple analysis. It could become more stimulating, healthier, more adult, more appealing to the very young, more targeted at the licensed on-trade, more of a celebration drink – the options are truly bewildering. Given enough time, money, ingenuity and determination, it would appear that Coke could go anywhere it wanted to – so how would we set about selecting its best route to further growth?

Before addressing this issue, we should try to understand the reasons for under-indexing (or under-performing). You can do this by answering these questions:

- Do we under-index because of a lack of awareness? Do people never think of us in this context?
- Do we under-index because of a lack of distribution? Potential customers may think of us but our products may not be available to them.
- Is there a problem with our image? People may be aware of us but we might have the wrong image for that occasion, need, group of people or channel.
- Should we vary our product or format? Even if we could change the image, is it the case that the product and/or the format (in the case of Coke, think packaging) frankly does not deliver?
- What trade-off implications are there? We could perhaps change the product and/or the image but only at the expense of some other fundamental, which would mean we will lose more than we gain.

Coke is the most successful branded drink on the planet because it has understood and, as far as possible, addressed the first four of these questions. It has driven awareness and distribution harder than anyone else. It has shown itself prepared to vary its format, its product and its image. It has done so within certain limits but has nevertheless been quite bold: Diet Coke targeted at women is one example. But to go for even more growth, to attack a redefined and bigger global beverages market, would force it into trade-offs that require it to address the strategic issue of portfolio.

That's because where there is a fundamental trade-off, there is a need for a different brand. For example, the changes necessary to get Coke to compete with drinks that present health as a key benefit might well compromise its huge market among people seeking refreshment or a treat – and that would certainly be a trade-off too far. So the only way for Coke to enter the health drinks market would be for it to offer a different brand. What, in theory would stop it doing this? The answer is that Coke has long had the mission of making its drink the number one global brand, rather than having the number one portfolio of brands. Which brings us to the next issue that needs to be addressed in our quest to 'do it different'.

3. Brand portfolios

What is the optimum number of brands that a company should have? And how should they be configured in the market? These are fundamental questions of strategy that can be answered by looking at what are known as 'brand portfolios'.

In marketing, we can talk about business portfolios, market portfolios and brand portfolios. The business portfolio represents investment choices across different businesses or markets which involve different competencies and which people see as unconnected. Unilever are in food and household products; Mars are in confectionery, human food and petfood; Yamaha are in motorbikes and pianos. With the exception of Yamaha, companies quite rightly deploy different brands for different markets or businesses. It is hard to see the connection between motorbikes and pianos so there is no logic in using the same brand. Like Yamaha, Rentokil also uses the same brand name across its business portfolio There is some connection between its outsourced business services, which are as diverse as waste disposal, pest control, buildings maintenance and supplying fresh plants and flowers for offices, but one would probably not naturally choose Rentokil as the brand for all of these.

A market portfolio represents choices within a market. However much we may try to differentiate the brands, they are seen as connected, and therefore at some abstract level as interchangeable. Coffee is different from a carbonated soft drink and people don't often actively choose between the two, or assume that a company that makes a good coffee knows how to make a good soft drink – although it might do. So one company might want to deploy totally different brands but another – Nestlé for example – might choose to make some connection at a branded level – Nescafé and Nestea.

Later in this chapter we cover the portfolio within or under a brand; this section deals with the strategic decisions about brand portfolio within a market. As Figure 2.4 illustrates, there are essentially three types of brand portfolio within a market – mono-brand, sun and planets, and stand-alone.

The sun and planets model makes an active choice that one brand will dominate. Nescafé is a classic example of this, with Nescafé itself as the dominant or 'sun' product, surrounded by planets such as Blend 37, Gold Blend and Alta Rica, each meeting the requirements of specific areas of the instant coffee market.

The stand alone – or multi-brand – model is rarely used in its pure form outside Proctor & Gamble, but the approach is to come to market with a

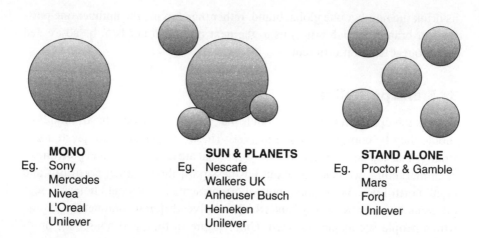

MONO
Eg. Sony
    Mercedes
    Nivea
    L'Oreal
    Unilever

SUN & PLANETS
Eg. Nescafe
    Walkers UK
    Anheuser Busch
    Heineken
    Unilever

STAND ALONE
Eg. Proctor & Gamble
    Mars
    Ford
    Unilever

Figure 2.4 The brand portfolio

selection of brands, each of which is designed to attack different parts of the market map. (There is a complication here illustrated by the example of Ford – you can choose to link the various brands through the parent or endorsement brand or not – but this will be covered under brand architecture.)

So how do you choose which model of brand portfolio is right for you? And if you go for more than one brand, how many brands is the right number? There is no right or wrong answer, and some companies, like Unilever, use variations of all three approaches. But the choice is really down to these five factors (Figure 2.5).

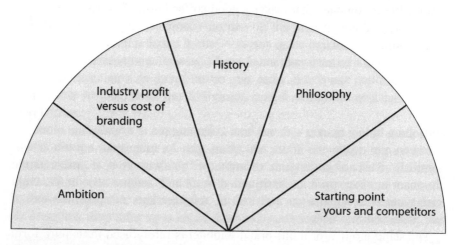

Figure 2.5 The portfolio fan

Let's start with ambition. How much of the market do you want? If it is a big market and one that is reasonably well developed, then a high market share, 30 per cent or more, is probably going to require more than one brand.

Next, how much does it cost to support a brand? And what is the available industry profit? These two simple questions can be answered very accurately with a great deal of analysis by a media buying agency and a management consultant, respectively. However, for strategic purposes, they can be answered quickly and cheaply. Ten years ago we conducted a study based on the analysis of the top 100 brands in the UK and in particular the most successful 20 to 30. The average marketing expenditure was roughly $10 million per brand. What this represented as a percentage of sales revenue varied a little, and was of course lower for the more successful brands (being more successful meant that they had higher revenues), but it was roughly 5 per cent. This figure would hold true for any of the big European markets, and is probably 7 to 10 times higher in the United States. Allowing for inflation, let's assume the cost of supporting a brand is roughly $15 million for a big European market and $100–150 million in the United States.

The available industry profit can be also be worked out approximately – just apply your net margin to the total market size. If, in a European market, the total available profit is $50 million and you are aiming for a third of it, then one brand would be the maximum. If it is $500 million and you want a quarter, maybe three to four brands are possible.

These calculations are deliberately simple and rough to illustrate the point that the number of brands is never that high, and your overwhelming reflex should be to have as few as possible.

The historical development and the philosophy of the business also play big parts in this kind of decision. Most companies start small, in one market, and if that market happens to be the United States or Japan, where there is an enormous domestic GDP to aim at, the company or brand will be quite big if it is successful. This tends to dictate the approach to international markets. A high percentage of the world's biggest brands are either Japanese or American. Japanese companies seem to have a philosophical preference for one brand: the company brand, such as Sony or Honda. Not all US businesses necessarily have the same philosophy, but strong domestic brands such as McDonald's or Levi's or Coke are built as mono-brands internationally.

The other aspect of historical development relates to this. If you have grown organically you will tend to have grown one brand. If you grow by acquisition you will by definition have acquired strong, often local brands. And as you will have paid a high price for the intangible assets (the brand), you won't be in a hurry to throw this away and replace it with your own brand. As a general rule, companies that have a lot of brands have grown by acquiring some of those brands.

And finally, let's go back to the starting point. What brands do you have? How are they positioned? What do they represent in the minds of people? How does this compare with the competition? Do you have the opportunity to consolidate around one or two brands, or are they all small and niche? Do you face a competitor with one dominant brand, which is always forcing you to look for more niche ways to attack?

There's no easy way to decide which model of brand portfolio is right for your company, but addressing the five factors above should certainly help. The truth is that most companies' brand portfolio is suboptimal in some way simply because they fail to analyse it clearly. The result is that a lot of companies have too many brands. Remember that the best number of brands to have is one, and hardly any companies successfully market more than three brands in any one market (if they have properly defined their market, that is). Brands are really like children: the more you have, the less active part you can play in their development. Or to switch analogies, portfolios are like gardens – if you take stuff out, what is left grows much better.

For many years a lot of companies have managed their brand portfolios according to the BCG model of stars, rising stars, problem children and cash cows. Figure 2.6 presents an alternative way of looking at the same thing, using five headings: drive aggressively, drive tactically, harvest tactically, harvest aggressively and exit.

	Ideal reality				
	Rule of thumb maximum	Ideal	Investment/ resource	Which brands currently?	What current resource given?
Invest/drive aggressively	1–2*	1	50–60%	A, B, C, D	40%
Invest/drive tactically and selectively	2–3	2	30–40%	E	5%
Harvest (tactically)	2–3	2	5–15%	F, G, H, I	50%
Harvest/milk aggressively	1–2	1	0–15%	J	5%
Exit/kill	?		0		

* Should include at least the mainstream or premium mainstream

Figure 2.6 Brand focus

Added Value often uses this diagram to help clients think through portfolio strategy. One exercise is to get people to give an approximate but honest assessment of how much resource in terms of a) people and b) marketing investment are needed for each category *before* they fill in the brands. When they then fill in the brands and add it all up, they find they have trebled the size of their marketing department and quadrupled their marketing budget. Now of course this could be the right decision, but it normally and correctly allows people to see they have too many brands.

On several occasions I have gone through portfolio strategy exercises with big businesses like Unilever and Frito Lay, where we have concluded that the portfolio was too big and it was then cut, not slightly or slowly, but very dramatically and quickly. In every case the business achieved growth, and much higher growth than it had imagined.

In most cases, we have found that the sun and planets model is best for businesses with more than one brand. In other words, choose one brand that you want to 'drive aggressively', grow it as big as possible, get the whole company behind it – in fact, bet the farm on it. Then orientate two or maybe three other brands around it, which you will 'drive tactically' to reach the places your 'sun' brand simply cannot penetrate. Any other brands in the portfolio should be ruthlessly 'harvested' and placed in the 'exit' column – with a timescale, of course.

I say that the sun and planets model is best 'in most cases', but maybe not in every case, as was shown by the experience of one of our clients, South African Breweries (now SAB Miller) in Poland. Its problem was that it had two candidates for the 'sun' brand role. One, Lech, was bigger, more mainstream and the obvious candidate. The other, Tyskie, was a smaller, regional beer from Silesia, not an area renowned for great beers unless you happen to be Silesian. Our recommendation was to harvest and as quickly as possible kill Tyskie, and put all the resources behind Lech. The company ignored our advice, and Tyskie is now the number one beer brand in Poland although it still has Lech. It was right. In a market like beer you can have more than one sun: it is a high frequency purchase market with more than enough room for two or three big mainstream brands, and if you are determined, two of them can be yours. But remember this is an exception to an otherwise good rule.

The portfolio strategy can and should be summarised on one chart using the Five W's.

This kind of map sets out very clearly the role for each brand in the portfolio and where it should be competing in the market. There will be overlap because brands have a bigger footprint than just the groups of people, situations, needs and places for which they are intended to be the best choice. Above all else, it allows us to be clear sighted and honest in our expectations of our brands' performance.

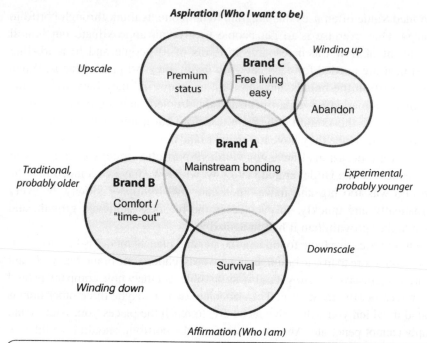

Figure 2.7 Portfolio strategy for long alcoholic drinks

But perhaps there is such a thing as being too honest about a brand. In the film *Crazy People,* Dudley Moore played a burnt out adman who ends up in an asylum, where he gets the inmates to start writing ads. They come up with brutally honest lines that capture what brands really are, rather than they way we would like to portray them. So Volvo is described as 'boxy but safe' and the Porsche line is 'You won't get laid in a Porsche but you might get laid with a Porsche.' The reason that such honesty doesn't make it into the final strategy document has a lot to do with the subject of our next section.

4. Brand positioning

We started this chapter with an insight about how to grow, how to win. We have used this to define our market, to segment it and to give ourselves a map, and so an idea of how to rewrite that map. We have considered our market portfolio and how many brands we need. We can now decide precisely, but also creatively and inspiringly, how to deploy those precious assets we call brands. Oh yes – and I am a monkey's uncle.

The implication of this whole book is that there is a neat Five 'I's process that starts with insight, and the implication of this chapter is that we move through to brand positioning in this logical order. But these are just frameworks – and frameworks are things that anyone can see right through. In the real world, nothing goes according to a plan: nothing starts where it's meant to, and, if it finishes at all, it never finishes in the place you expect it to. But that doesn't mean frameworks aren't valuable. They are there to provide reference points for comparison and yardsticks to measure progress. The start and end points in any framework are simply arbitrary markers of convenience.

As was said in the very first chapter, the Five 'I's process can start anywhere. I chose to start with insight, but for many marketers, it will start right here, in the middle of Chapter 2 – with brand positioning. After all, the vast majority of marketing strategy starts with a statement like, 'We have this brand but it is not delivering to our expectations.'

These expectations are normally not clearly defined, but let's put that aside for now. The first thing to do here is to understand what the brand is all about and how it might be developed; that is to say, how its positioning can create more growth. In the process of examining this, we may or may not realise that we need to work back through market definition, segmentation, portfolio strategy and so on. In fact, if you look at the Levi's Engineered Jeans case study in Appendix 2, that is exactly how that story began.

The reader may have noticed that at no point so far has a definition of a brand been attempted. The simple reason for this is that it has all been said before. Perhaps the best summary was given in Jeremy Bullmore's recent article, 'Posh Spice and Persil'. Jeremy has spent the last 50 years building great brands like Persil, so I make no apologies for quoting the following chunky extract.[3]

Thirteen disconcerting facts about brands

1. *Products are made and owned by companies. Brands, on the other hand, are made and owned by people, by the public, by consumers.*
2. *A brand image belongs not to a brand, but to those who have knowledge of that brand.*
3. *The image of a brand is a subjective thing. No two people, however similar, hold precisely the same view of the same brand.*
4. *A global brand – that highest of all ambitions for many CEOs – is therefore a contradiction in terms and an impossibility.*
5. *People come to conclusions about brands as a result of an uncountable*

number of different stimuli, many of which are way outside the control or even influence of the product's owner.

6. *Brands – unlike products – are living, organic entities. They change, however imperceptibly, every single day.*

7. *Much of what influences the value of a brand lies in the hands of its competitors.*

8. *The only way to begin to understand the nature of brands is to strive to acquire a facility which only the greatest of novelists possess and which is so rare it has no name.*

9. *The study of brands – in itself a relatively recent discipline – has generated a level of jargon that not only prompts deserved derision among financial directors but also provides some of the most entertaining submissions in Pseuds' Corner.*

10. *It is universally accepted that brands are a company's most valuable asset, yet there is no universally accepted method of measuring that value.*

11. *The only time you can be sure of the value of your brand is just after you have sold it.*

12. *It is becoming more and more apparent that, far from brands being hierarchically inferior to companies, only if companies are managed as brands can they hope to be successful.*

13. *And as if all this were not enough, in one of the most important works about brands published last year, the author says this: 'Above all, I found I had to accept that effective brand communications ... involves processes which are uncontrolled, disordered, abstract, intuitive ... and frequently impossible to explain other than with the benefit of hindsight'.*

Point number 9 refers to the jargon associated with brand positioning, and I must hold my hand up as guilty for making a significant contribution to this cornucopia of brand positioning tools that include icebergs, wheels, charters, gestalts, essences, keys, triangles, stars and all manner of other mnemonic devices. Not only did I help create Added Value's Brand Bullseye, but also several adaptations of this that are used as proprietary techniques by some very large companies. By way of atonement for contributing to a movement that made brands more complicated for non-marketers (and probably for some marketers too), this section will simplify and demystify.

The very first positioning project we ever did at Added Value was for Coopers & Lybrand (now merged and part of PricewaterhouseCoopers). It was at the time of the first round of consolidation in the accountancy industry. and Coopers & Lybrand were in danger of being left standing at the dance, as all around them merged or discussed the possibility. It faced the prospect of falling out of the Big Four firms and therefore out of an automatic place on a pitch list. The enlightened Senior Partner, Sir Brandon Gough, decided it needed to look at its brand positioning – that is to say, something that expressed its point of difference as a brand. Unilever was a big client of theirs which knew something about brands, and my partner and I were ex Unilever, so we got the job.

In the 12 years since this first project, Added Value has gone on to become one of the experts in brand positioning with a tool, Bullseye, that is one of the most comprehensive around. If there were a world league table of brand positioners, it would be top or near the top, having now positioned more than 350 big brands around the globe. But note the 'one of' – there are now many, many others who offer the same service.

As it happened, events overtook the Coopers & Lybrand repositioning project, as the firm merged first with part of the old Deloitte Touche firm and eventually with Price Waterhouse. But I'm still rather proud of that first positioning proposal of ours. In fact, when we presented it to the senior partners forum, it prompted a round of applause. One partner even came up to me afterwards and said it was the first time that anyone had ever explained what the firm aspired to be in a way that he could understand and found motivating. Recalling this, I decided to go back and look at how I had explained brands and positioning, and also to dig out the early prototype tool I had used. It was very simple, deliberately so, because I had to present it to a room full of what were effectively 250 finance directors, who were very smart and suspicious of marketers. This is what I said:

- Brands are a bundle of shared values and associations – like a star in a soap opera. The character comes across consistently to you and the other 10 million people who watch them. You all understand their strengths and weaknesses and how they will react in a certain situation.
- Brands are a mark of pride – this is what we do and what we stand for. We have applied our unique signature so you can recognise us and recommend us to a friend.
- Brands are therefore a simplifier of choice – they are useful to prospective buyers.
- Brands are differentiated; they have competitive advantage.
- A brand positioning is a summary of all of this, a summary of competitive advantage.
- Picture the typical client, in the typical situation, talking to a friend who is considering changing to another firm of accountants. The friend asks, 'You use Coopers & Lybrand. What are they like?' Now imagine that you have a gun against this client's head: what would you like him or her to say? The answer is your brand positioning.

At the end of it, this was the brand positioning statement that we came up for Coopers & Lybrand:

Market Positioning Statement

Coopers & Lybrand see things from the businessperson's point of view. They know the importance of competitive advantage and understand why people are always a company's greatest asset. Their business solutions offer an integrated combination of the best accountancy and the best consultancy but they also know that they're only as good as the relationships that communicate them and the people who implement them.

Over the years we have made a few useful additions to our market positioning technique, but the main points are these.

- The "typical client' is now a pen portrait of the ideal buyer, described in the situation for which your brand would be the ideal choice. It is in fact a summary of your insight about the market, what it means to people, how it segments or could be segmented and where you are targeting.
- The target response remains as it was originally designed – what a client would say about you on a good day.
- There is a 'Bullseye', which is the recipe for the cake. It answers five basic questions:
  1. What other choices would you expect to be considered alongside?
  2. What are the key benefits you offer? Most brands offer more than one benefit that should be listed. They also conform to certain market generic benefits: for example, airlines are safe (we hope). These are important and – watch out – they can become discriminating benefits, but for the most part they are not and should be listed separately.
  3. What are your values and personality? What does this brand believe in? What kind of person would it be?
  4. Why should people believe this? What proof or substantiation does the brand offer?
  5. What is the summary proposition? Of all the benefits, values, personality, reasons to believe, which would you want to be foremost in the prospective buyers' minds? (It helps to think 'first, best, only'.)
- Another product that we have alchemically distilled is what we call 'the brand essence'. This is the word or phrase that encapsulates the brand and summarises the key thought behind it. For example:

Kelloggs	=	Sunshine vitality
Disney	=	Childhood magic
Microsoft	=	Empowerment
Nike	=	Self-esteem through self-expression in sport
Virgin	=	Richard Branson = Robin Hood

There is no doubt that the pursuit of this 'brand essence' forces a profound appraisal of the brand and takes you to new levels of understanding – but it is a potentially very self-indulgent exercise. As Jeremy Bullmore says, to do it well requires a facility 'which only the greatest of novelists possess and is so rare it has no name'!

- We also devised a 'Brand Calling Card' – a visual summary of the brand's associations in the minds of people: the way it is recognised and especially the things that bring its uniqueness to mind. It could be the logo, a scene from a famous ad, even a colour. Actually, this doesn't even have to be visual. It can also involve noise, smell, touch – although this can make it much harder to photocopy.
- Finally, there is the 'action matrix'. This is really an exercise in wishful thinking – a way of describing the desired destination for your brand, rather than its starting point. It invites you to list the places where you would like the positioning to take you. In other words, what action do you need to get from the position you currently occupy in people's minds to the place you really want to be?

Having covered all the points above, think back to your market map and run through your answers to the Five 'W's again. Just answer the five simple questions:

- What is the brand?
- Who is it best for?
- When – in which situations?
- Why?
- Where – in which places?

We started with a fairly simple technique for positioning – the target buyer response – which we have elaborated through a number of tools and techniques. And there is a risk in doing this: the risk that the process becomes too mechanistic, too much from the right side of the brain. The benefit is that this lays bare the competitive advantage of the brand so that a) it can be understood and applied to the innovation, impact and investment return stages and b) the assumptions can be challenged and/or changed. After all, if we don't list them, we can't check them.

However, positioning is fundamentally about inspiration. We work hard to understand the brand – what it is and what it can be – in order to inspire us. The basic questions posed are very simple, and you will have noticed that they are very similar to the fundamental questions at the heart of strategy. It does not matter what technique or tool you use as long as it covers the ground, as long as it is thorough and it involves both analysis and creativity. But note that this can be a lengthy process. I have never seen positioning done well in less than three months, and more often it can take six.

The only criteria to apply are:

- Is it clear?
- Is it based on truth?
- Does it stretch?
- Is it differentiated from competing brands?
- Is it inspiring?

The fundamental point Jeremy Bullmore makes in his article is that brands succeed if they achieve long-term fame, not just short-term preference. This means that your brand needs to become a character in people's lives; a walk-on part just won't do. But to achieve that it needs to be both distinctive and memorable. A brand that just does what it's supposed to do is simply not working hard enough.

5. Brand extension and architecture

I have lost count of the analogies I have already used or borrowed for brands. It is a soap opera star, a plant in a garden, a cake with a recipe – well, it is also a building that can be extended and requires architecture. If this sounds complicated, let's make it even more complex. Here are just a few of the many types of brands that experts have defined:

Niche
Power
Umbrella
Challenger
Star
Lifestyle
Affinity
Service
Product
Sub-brands

Master-brands
Brand extensions

Some are reasonably self-explanatory, some are very opaque. So now let's simplify this a bit. There are in fact two types of brands and three levels of branding (which, of course, adds up to five). The two types of brands relate to the 'What? and the 'Why?' – what a brand is, versus why you buy it. The three levels of branding are: the endorsement brand, the purchase brand and versions of the brand.

Let's start with the two types of brand, based on 'What?' and 'Why?' Some brands are very much defined by what they are, their physical format. Audi is a German car. British Airways is a very British airline. Coke is a cola drink. On the other hand, other brands are based on a more intangible 'Why?' factor. Virgin, for example, is an iconoclastic consumer champion. Nike is a celebration of sport and its opportunities for creativity, self-expression and self-esteem. Body Shop is belief in the environment and fair trade. The reasons behind all this lie in the history of the brand: some brands have done one thing very well for decades, and the personality and values of the brand have grown out of this, with 'some help' from the brand communications. The reason for saying, some help, is that brands will also develop personalities with no help from communications. Ariel detergent has a very clear, no-nonsense personality, which comes purely from its excellent functional performance of tough stain removal. Other brands have developed a wider range of products and services as the expression of their values and beliefs, and the brand communications have rather more quickly and deliberately held out those values with an implicit invitation to 'come and join us'.

For the sake of clarity let's call these product-based brands versus values-based brands, but we recognise that this is shorthand and that all brands are a mixture of the two. Being more product-led, the 'What?', or being more values-led, the 'Why?', says nothing about potential – Coke is a very big brand, Body Shop or Virgin are relatively smaller. But it does give an indication of the potential to grow through range extension per se. For example, it is hard to imagine a Coke fragrance but easy to imagine a Body Shop range of drinks.

As Coke, or Mercedes, or Guinness have demonstrated, you can build a big brand with huge growth potential by being product-led. Range extension is not the only route to growth, and indeed can be a dangerous one, for the simple reason that every expression of the brand must deliver, and the more you extend, the more you risk moving into areas in which you have no competence. Better to be known to be great at one thing, than average at lots of things. However, brands are such valuable assets, requiring high investment to maintain and grow, that it is very tempting to leverage the brand by extending it.

The golden rules of brand extension are very simple but rarely adhered to. They can be expressed as a virtuous circle. You should extend into a new category if by doing so a) you bring a new solution or opportunity to the category and b) you strengthen your existing business.

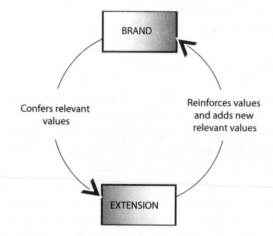

Figure 2.8 The virtuous circle

Brands, like Sony, with the potential to extend will have the five features shown in Figure 2.9.

	SONY
1. They are very good at what they currently do.	✔
2. They stand for something in people's minds, a broad benefit and/or a set of values, that is extendable, rather than a more specific product-led benefit that is not.	✔
3. They have a clear sense of solving a problem or creating an opportunity for buyers in the new category, rather than solving a problem or creating an opportunity for them as a business.	✔
4. There is some track record of similar brands extending. (A simple point but it is hard to extend a fizzy drink because no-one has ever done it, but much easier to extend a luxury goods brand because lots of people have done it).	✔
5. They have a name that is open-ended.	✔

Figure 2.9 Brands with the potential to extend

So Sony is a very extendable brand. It makes great products and it stands for design and technology, which have broad appeal. People are also used to seeing technology companies extend their range, and Sony is a great brand name that means something, nothing and potentially anything, all at the same time.

A few years ago, we looked at the possibilities of extending the British Airways brand. It was a difficult time for the company: they were in the process of changing their tail fins, the staff had been on strike and Virgin had established a better long-haul product. The marketing director worked for a CEO who was a lawyer. They had seen what Virgin had done and thought British Airways could do the same. We deep dived into the brand and came up with all sorts of weird and wonderful ideas for range extensions, all of which bombed out in research for some very simple reasons. First, in the research we showed concepts when we really needed fantastic prototypes; the second problem was that British Airways scored a negative in response to each of the five statements above.

Actually British Airways is a very fine airline, but it's in an industry that is structurally flawed and in an environment designed to ensure you fail at least some of the time (think: weather, air traffic controllers, airports). The idea we came up with was for British Airways to change its name to BA and to start by trying to own the celebration of travel as a life-enhancing, business-enhancing experience. Then, they should concentrate on extending only in the travel arena where we were certain they could offer new, different, better solutions. It might have worked. They have launched some new products and services but the marketing director left, the CEO left and events overtook them somewhat. I remain a loyal BA customer and optimistic that the fantastic service you receive in the plane can yet be leveraged.

As a simple summary, when you contemplate extending a brand, first reassure yourself that you have or are doing everything you can to grow what you've got. You almost certainly are not. Second, think **why**, not why not.

If you do decide to extend, you have then to choose names for the extensions and decide what relationship you want them to have with the 'parent' brand. Often the extensions are called sub-brands, which is as motivating as describing a direct report as a sub-manager or anyone as sub-human.

If we start with real people in the real world, it is clear there are only three levels of branding. First there is the thing you ask for – the purchase brand. Second, there is the endorsement brand – normally the name of the big company that owns the brand. So, for example, the Galaxy is endorsed by Ford, whereas Coke is not endorsed at all. Sometimes the relationship between the endorsement brand and the purchase brand is so close that it is hard to tell which is which: many people would say 'I drive a Galaxy' and assume other people know it's a Ford.

Then there are versions of the brand. Diet Coke is a version of Coke. Versions tend to be denoted by a descriptor: in this case, 'Diet'. Because it is so descriptive and generic, simply asking for a Coke would not get you a Diet Coke. By design, or sometimes just through prolonged usage, descriptors can become ownable descriptors. 'I drive a GTI' tells me it is a Golf GTI and no one else's, and so distinctive was the car that it became pretty much a purchase brand in its own right. The acid test of this is that you can say, 'I am not really a VW or a Golf person but I like the GTI and I love the Beetle.' You couldn't say, 'I really like the 5 series but I don't really like BMW.'

Endorsement brand		Ford	VW	Kelloggs	
Purchase brand	Coca-Cola	Galaxy	Beetle	Frosties	The Gap
Versions of the brand	Diet Coke	Galaxy LX	Convertible	Chocolate Frosties	Baby Gap

Figure 2.10 Levels of brand

Deciding whether the brand is to be endorsed, and if extending the brand, what to call the extensions or versions and what relationship they should have with the brand, are strategic choices that have implications. The simple and most frequently discussed implication is investment.

The theory goes that you should put all your investment in just one place, behind one brand. This suggests that it's best to use simple descriptors for versions of the brand which keep it as close to the parent as possible. If you distance every version from the parent, then each one will require its own investment. Endorsements should, in theory, be avoided. This is because if you have an endorsement, you will need to invest in that as well.

However, this is less true than might at first appear. The endorsement brand investment can be amortised across a lot of brands, and it will comprise the kind of things that you should be doing anyway (making great products, managing your corporate brand). Furthermore, if a version of a brand has a good story to tell – and it should do – you will need to spend money to communicate this. An old Added Value study showed that the same was spent on the successful launch of a new brand as a version of an existing brand. This is not to say that there are not some economies for the tightly formed mono-brand, just that they should not be exaggerated.

The second implication is more important and comes back to the virtuous circle. If you want it to be virtuous it needs to be tight.

So, having been through five ways of 'doing it different', let's finish this chapter by bringing it all together with some specific ideas on how to win.

WINNING STRATEGIC IDEAS

Let's imagine we are trying to enter a food market. It doesn't matter which type of food market, although we will have made it our first task to define or redefine the market. This is going to be a simple example to illustrate some simple ideas.

When you look at the basic needs segmentation of a market, there is often a simple triangle that can be drawn which isolates the basic parameters of choice that face people. In cars it might be practical, fun and solid (that is, safe and reliable). In grocery shopping it might be range, service and fresh produce. For food, the triangle might look like Figure 2.11.

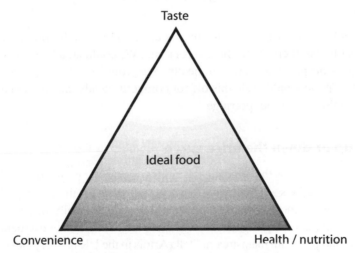

Figure 2.11 The triangle of choice for food

Think of these as the Holy Grail. Any car that offered great looks, reliability, safety, was fun to drive, could carry lots of people and luggage, and had great resale value would be a winner. Any supermarket that carried the full range, with great personal service and wonderful fresh foods, would be packed every day of the week. And any food that tasted great, could be prepared in just a couple of minutes and was good for you, would be very successful. The egg has done pretty well.

To some extent these factors are trade-offs. It is not easy to be fun and practical and solid. Or to carry a big range and offer great personal service. Or to be tasty, good for you and quick. But they are not always trade-offs. You can be practical and solid – Volvo is. You can offer great service and great fresh produce – Waitrose in the UK does. You can be convenient and good for you – yoghurt is. But these parameters allow you to map where all the brands sit in the market and to see that the big brand leader is out in front because it is, in the case of food, tasty, convenient and relatively healthy.

So our job is to attack the egg – the brand leader in food offering taste first, but in a convenient form and with lots of nutritional value. How do we attack? There are five potential strategies.

Full frontal

We could just go for eggs – head on with a new food that tastes better, is even more convenient and healthier. We could call this new food, soup.

Focus

We can select one of the benefits and focus single-mindedly on it. An egg is quite healthy but there is the cholesterol issue. We could attack this benefit and beat eggs – no pun intended – on health. We would want some convenience and taste but we would trade this off for competitive advantage on health. We could call this new food, porridge.

Move up or down the price curve

Everyone understands the principle the more you pay, the more you get. In addition to the Five W's – what, who, why, when, where – there is a 'V', value segmentation. In most developed markets there are normally three segments, economy, standard and premium. In some there are five, the other two being super premium, and premium mainstream. Stella Artois in the UK is a very clever brand. It has built its whole positioning on being premium and using this as the 'evidence' of its quality, where in fact it is only marginally more expensive than other mainstream beers and often cheaper on promotion. To be the brand that most people are prepared to pay a little more for is the most profitable place to be. Super premium is self explanatory and exists in many markets, particularly connoisseur markets or areas of conspicuous consumption like wine, watches or cars, because there is always a group of 'experts' or super rich who want to pay more.

So we could attack by going below them on price with a product that offers a little less taste, health and convenience but is much cheaper. We could call this a potato. Or we could go way above eggs with a premium offer that is much tastier, healthier and convenient. It would need a very distinctive look, some heritage and a decadent name. We could call it, caviar.

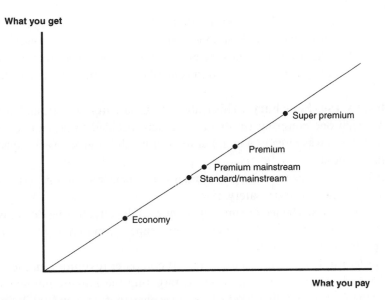

Figure 2.12 The price/value curve

Resegment

Eggs are for anyone, any time, any place. We could resegment the market and go after a particular group of people, or occasion or channel or any combination of these. We could target a particular group of people who are not so committed to eggs – children. And we could focus on an occasion where nutrition is important – breakfast. By creating this new segment we could perfect our offering to be the best choice for kids at breakfast with exactly the taste they like. We could call this, breakfast cereal.

Change the rules

We could introduce a new benefit, challenge the rules and market assumptions, or redefine an existing benefit. We could make a food that was refreshing and stimulating, a food that would make you lose your inhibitions, that was so different it was even consumed in a different way. A food you could drink. We could call this, beer. Or we could redefine this benefit, health and nutrition. We could take one aspect of nutrition, make it sound more appealing possibly to particular people on particular occasions. This new spin on health and nutrition could be – energy. And we could call our food – nuts.

And that, ladies and gentlemen, is strategy from soup to nuts.

Earlier we heard how Michael Porter defined two types of strategy – 'do it better or do it different'. The first approach, 'full frontal', corresponds to 'do it better'; the other four strategies are all ways of 'doing it different'.

Any case study you have ever read fits one of the five strategies listed above.

- **Tesco versus Sainsburys.** This is the classic case of a 'full frontal attack' in which one company (in this case Tesco) decided to do exactly what Sainsburys was already doing, but to do it much better in every aspect of the business.
- **Volvo.** Volvo exemplifies the strategy of focusing on one particular benefit – in their case, safety.
- **Häagen Dazs.** The ice cream maker showed the effectiveness of moving up the price curve and creating a new super premium segment in an already existing market.
- **Apple.** Apple kick-started the personal computer revolution in the early 1980s by resegmenting the market, targeting the home computer user for the first time with a product that was easy to access and totally user-friendly.
- **American Express.** American Express completely changed the rules for charge cards, by associating its card with status and cosmopolitan living at a time when it hadn't crossed the minds of any of its competitors to do so.

And to be sure many case studies, including all of the above, involve combinations of these strategies.

The point has already been made that an idea cannot be evaluated except by implementing it. However, you can evaluate your assumptions and you should make a choice from among options. Most businesses write some form of a three or five year plan, and the plans are almost always a 'hockey stick' – however, tough things are in the short term, the plan always says they will get better. What is never clear, and I make this statement after having read a great many of these plans, is, 'What's the big idea?' If nothing else, this section should inspire you to write your strategy simply and clearly.

When Frito Lay merged its two snacks businesses in the UK into one business, Walkers Snack Foods, I worked with Dale Morrison and his senior team on their first five year strategy. By the time it was presented in Dallas it was a deck of 30 or more charts, but the strategy was on one piece of paper and comprised just six bullet points:

- Focus on Walkers and make it a mega brand by owning the category benefit – irresistible taste.
- Invest in Walkers potato chip product quality to achieve a noticeable difference, support a premium price, and reinvest the margin in brand support.
- Cut the portfolio to create focus and take out complexity cost.
- Create category news – specifically launch Doritos and build a new mainstream corn chips segment targeted at teens.
- Build a stronger sales force and win the war in the stores.
- Upgrade the marketing team.

It was a great strategy – full frontal, changing the rules, resegmenting. It correctly identified the assets to be strengthened and addressed the weaknesses in the portfolio. More importantly it was brilliantly executed. Walkers is now the most admired and by most objective criteria, in particular its growth record, the most successful FMCG business in the UK.

A great strategy inspires you to action, to change things, above all, to innovate....

THE STUFF THAT GETS IN THE WAY OF IDEAS

1. There are no burning platforms or glorious goals

If the advice in this book comes across as bordering on the bloody obvious, ask yourself why so few people lead healthy lives. Yes, there is lots of conflicting evidence on precisely which diet and which exercise regime is the best, just like there are lots of consultants and business books all of which claim to have *the* answer. But we all know that eating less, eating fewer fatty foods, following a balanced diet, not smoking and drinking responsibly, plus 45 minutes exercise three times a week, will make us feel and look better and will prolong our lives. Surely these are objectives we can all sign on for, just like business growth. Now ask yourself why people mostly don't do all these things, and why sometimes they do. They mostly don't do it for two reasons – they don't care enough about the objective so they won't make any trade-offs, and/or they have low self-esteem. The reason they do it is always some form of a burning platform or glorious goal – they need to escape from a situation that is becoming unbearable or they are inspired to achieve an ambition. Perhaps they enter a marathon for which they have to get fit. Or they lose a partner or get a partner or are desperate for a partner. Perhaps a doctor, using some new KPI, such as cholesterol levels, tells them they will die if they don't follow his advice. Perhaps they want to start a family.

Strategy is not only stretch, it is stretching away from a burning platform, from some situation that is deeply unsatisfactory. Or it is stretch towards a glorious goal – a place that is fabulously attractive. It is easy to spot a business that has some sense of burning platform or glorious goal, and it tends to have great ideas that it will implement – or it will die in the process.

2. Long-winded strategy documents

Most strategy documents – and I have read a great many – are long, boring and obtuse. A good strategy can be captured on one piece of paper, a few simple statements. It always is when the case study is written or the conference speech is delivered. This is essential to address the next point.

3. Poor communication

Even in these days of empowerment, it is not necessary to share every detail of the strategy with every employee or partner or trade customer. It is necessary to share the overall strategy and their role in it, and it is necessary to do this over and over again. Lee Iacocca puts his success down to his skill as a communicator, and this is true of many business winners. For strategy to work, it has to be understood, and that requires repeated communication of a simple message.

4. Too many agendas

Companies are only successful when their leadership team is honest about its real agenda. And yet I have done countless stakeholder interviews in which it has become clear that there is a major clash of not one, but several conflicting agendas: people are thinking of promotion, or a knighthood, or the chance to keep a factory open or screw a colleague – you name it. Successful sporting teams win because they have one agenda – it's a lesson that most businesses still have to learn.

5. Poor implementation

Porter was mostly right, there are two strategies: do it better and do it different, but in terms of implementation it is always 'do it different'. Most strategies fail because this is not appreciated and not followed through. Successful leaders are not necessarily smarter than less successful ones, they are simply better implementers. If you had a good time at college and went on to be successful you always think your college was the best college. The fact is you have no basis for comparison, you simply picked a college and made it a success for you. It is the same with strategy. Like college, you can never test a strategy, you can only test the assumptions it is based on (has it got a good football team? a high ratio of girls to boys, or vice versa? good alumni?). The best strategy is the one you implement successfully, and you implement it successfully because you were prepared to make changes. Every strategy should be accompanied by a simple chart that lists what, as a result of this strategy, you will stop doing, start doing and continue to do, hopefully with more urgency than ever before.

CHAPTER 3

Innovation

There is a great scene in the film *Apollo 13*. Disaster has struck the mission, the air supply system has gone wrong and the astronauts, in orbit, are rapidly running out of oxygen. Their only hope lies with the ingenuity of the NASA technical team on the ground. The boffins are duly called into a room and a clutter of objects is emptied onto the table.

'This is the equipment the guys up there have available to them,' they are told. 'You gotta figure out a way of getting the oxygen system working again and you got two hours to do it.' A clear brief, a compelling goal, personal commitment within the context of a team ethic – the perfect conditions for innovation to flourish.

And yet these conditions are rarely found in business life. Too often we treat innovation as a haphazard process best suited to a loose, chaotic 'anything goes' environment. We picture it as something entirely separate from a company's normal systems – and marvel as it sprints in from 'left field' confounding all expectations. Or we see it as the product of serendipity coming from 'out of the blue' with little in the way of precedent or explanation. Indeed, in some companies, lucky folk get paid good money to do 'blue-sky thinking', as if scanning the empty sky for Unidentified Innovative Objects were the surest way to innovate to success.

In the Five 'I's process, innovation is the result of great strategic ideas inspired by a combination of inspirational insights. Very simply, innovation is an idea, driven by an insight – that happens. All innovation is innovation for a purpose. It should solve a problem or create a new opportunity for a buyer, but it should also fit some more precisely defined strategy. In fact, in most cases, it should even have a written brief. And it just so happens that all meaningful innovation leads to just one end: profitable growth.

Innovative ideas, even good innovative ideas, are rarely in short supply. It is almost never the case that a competitor comes up with something that no one has thought of before. Someone, somewhere in your organisation has almost certainly had the same idea, but it was simply never implemented. The only reason that companies fail to innovate is that they don't have the insights or the strategic ideas to enable that innovation to occur. This could be an explanation for the way that innovation appears to move forward in sudden flurries of activity, preceded – and often followed – by periods of plodding, uncreative torpor.

Take the case of the humble tea bag, which had once itself been a major innovation. Strangely, after its introduction to the market it was, for many years, left untouched. Perhaps it was so obviously a great innovation in comparison with loose tea that people just forgot to ask how it could be improved. Instead, they focused on the quality of the tea in the bag. Then one day, Tetley introduced the round tea bag, which improved the taste because it allowed the tea to infuse better. Unilever responded with the triangular tea bag, and before you knew it there were drawstrings too, so you could squeeze out the last drop of flavour and throw the bag away without so much as a drip on the kitchen floor. Apparently, out of nowhere had come a modest revolution in tea bags.

But of course those innovations hadn't come out of nowhere. In all likelihood, they'd been presented by some bright-eyed young researcher many years before, but they'd been tucked away in a dusty file because they didn't seem relevant at the time. Sadly, all too often, business innovation is a tale of lonely heroism and bloody-mindedness, as stubborn individuals struggle to have their brilliant innovations adopted by blinkered, backward-looking bureaucracies. British industry is notoriously bad at harnessing innovation, as inventors from Barnes Wallis to James Dyson will testify. But one of the most famous stories of great innovation and stubborn individualism comes from the United States – with the tale of the Post-it note. What most people seem to remember about the Post-it note is that it came from an experiment into new types of super glue that went wrong – the result of serendipity, a bit like the discovery of penicillin. In fact, from our point of view, this is the least interesting thing about it.

The real story is told by Gifford Pichot III in his excellent book, *Intrapreneuring*,[4] where he explains how people can be entrepreneurs within an organisation. The man behind the Post-it note was Art Fry, and what he went through to get his innovation onto the market exemplifies all the characteristics of the true innovator. Here are some of the highlights of the story that Pichot tells:

- Fry's insight came from using small bits of loose paper to mark pages in his hymn book during Sunday church. They always fell out.
- He had to wait his turn to get use of the pilot plant to make the prototypes. When it came he worked 40 hours straight.
- In response to the indifference of his colleagues he left Post-it notes on their desks for them to use so they became advocates. He put a lot of his limited budget into an internal sales aid for the project. The Post-it notes failed in the first round of research but he learnt from the failure and battled on.
- When the engineers told him it would take six months to build a machine to make the Post-it note, he went home and built it himself in a weekend.
- He admits his big problem was that the innovation was so original that he did not have the words to describe it.

What is not discussed in Pichot's book is that Art's company, 3M, has never exploited the full potential of the Post-it. It was launched as a new and convenient way of leaving messages – which, of course, it is – but the company completely failed to realise any of its many other uses. So, it wasn't marketed as a creative tool, or a mini filing system or a display aid, and indeed it was a very long time before it was offered in any other shapes, sizes or colours. It was also never properly branded, which meant that its name was allowed to become a generic term. The lack of brand value in the Post-it name allowed competitors to move in with identical products as soon as the opportunity arose.

The facts are that Art Fry should not have had to work so hard and the Post-it note should have been even more successful than it has been. Why it worked out like it did is anyone's guess. My own theory is that like a lot of innovation, the process of giving birth was so exhausting that the parents forgot that raising the child to be a great person is the point of the exercise. But this should take nothing away from Art Fry's work and his dogged persistence in making sure that his baby got to market. Gifford Pichot sums up his achievements in his 'Ten Commandments for the Intrapreneur':

The Intrapreneur's 10 Commandments

1. Come to work each day willing to be fired.

2. Circumvent any orders aimed at stopping your dream.

3. Do any job needed to make your project work, regardless of your job description.

4. Find people to help you.

5. Follow your intuition about the people you choose, and work only with the best.

6. Work underground as long as you can – publicity triggers the corporate immune mechanism.

7. Never bet on a race unless you are running in it.

8. Remember it is easier to ask for forgiveness than for permission.

9. Be true to your goals, but be realistic about the ways to achieve them.

10. Honor your sponsors.

But of course it is a travesty that innovative individuals should come to work each day willing to be fired. And truly innovative companies – they're the ones that have achieved the solid gold, top-line growth we've talked about – are the ones that expect every employee to obey the commandments above, with the exception of the first and sixth, obviously. In fact, innovation – the desire to make things different and better – is akin to a religion, an act of faith that cannot be turned on and off. If there is a clear sense of purpose, a continual search for insight and a consistent appetite for innovation, then innovation will surely happen.

One of the obstacles to this is that innovation has become synonymous with product innovation. But that's utterly wrong. Innovation is 360 degrees. And if you don't know what I mean, look around you. If innovation is about doings things different and doing things better, then it applies to everything – it doesn't matter whether it's your supply chain, your trade terms, how you run a meeting or where you have your Christmas party. This is not an invitation to change everything just for the sake of it. But, like the patterns discussed earlier in the section on semiotics, the trick is to recognise when to respect something and when to challenge it.

The Magnum ice cream was a huge global success for the first ten years of its life, but after that it cooled off, with only flavour variations as the 'innovations'. Magnum seemed to be locked into its product format – everything had to be big, covered in thick real chocolate and on a stick. Only when the company recognised that the true equities were sensual absorption and personal indulgence (covered, of course, in thick chocolate), did it begin truly to innovate with new formats targeted at new occasions – which led the brand back to the path of renewed growth.

Even if you decide not to change absolutely everything all at once (and you'd be well advised not to) there's always something that can be improved. The really great businesses and brands are never satisfied and never rest on their laurels. Walkers and Frito Lay know they make a great potato chip but they will never believe that it is as good as it could be, and they will never stop investing in bringing improvements and innovations to the market.

Innovation is also exhausting. It requires the kind of passion and tenacity it takes to win the Super Bowl, and by that I mean not just the Super Bowl itself but the many games over a long hard season that it takes to get to the final. Many books and articles have been written about the need for passion, grit and teamwork to drive successful innovation, and the sport analogy has been used so many times it is a cliché. But like most clichés it is true. Every successful innovation project I have ever worked on had a clear goal and a team of committed people who stuck with the project. And every failed project (of which there have also been many) was characterised by a lack of passion, a lack of commitment and a lack of purpose. The ideas are really the easy bit – innovation, making those ideas happen, is very hard.

INNOVATION PROCESS OVERVIEW

As I mentioned, innovation is a 360 degree process: it should be about everything that happens in a company. But in this next section, we're going to focus on the type of product innovation that builds naturally on the Insight and Idea stages of the Five 'I's process. And we'll attempt to make the conception, confinement and birth of our innovative new product a bit less exhausting than it often is.

Figure 3.2 shows the typical programme of work that would be undertaken for an innovation project. We are going to concentrate on five aspects of this.

1. The innovation matrix
2. Funnels and charters
3. Ideas generators
4. The role of research and the power of the prototype
5. Staying on track and running the team.

So, first, let's put our innovation project into context.

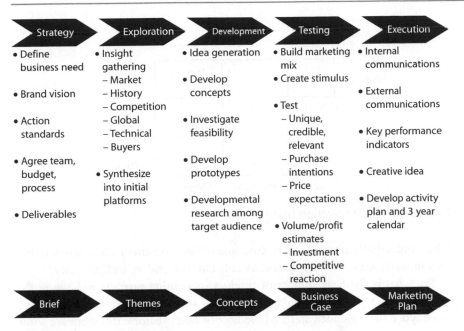

Figure 3.2 Typical programme of work for an innovation project

1. The innovation matrix

Any specific innovation should be part of a bigger innovation matrix that maps all the projects, both active and potential, that are intended to deliver growth in line with the overall strategy.

There are various versions of this kind of matrix knocking around. McKinsey talk about the three horizons of growth, and their studies of successful businesses prove the intuitive point that it is a good idea to have innovation that balances the near-in and the far-out. If everything is over the horizon you never get there, but if everything is right in front of your nose you don't progress very far either. Perhaps the simplest way to say this is that good businesses balance the short, medium and long term and invest in all three.

Figure 3.3 is our version of an innovation matrix.

Of course, the ideal is innovation that makes a huge impact and is really easy to achieve. But life is rarely that simple. This means that it is the CEO's job to a) ensure that the matrix is full and balanced and b) to keep it under constant review. He or she should continually challenge the innovation team by asking what extra investment could be made to advance any of the projects, especially the high impact ones. Impatience is a good quality in a CEO. Look at Sony. Just three years ago we turned to them for TVs, hi-fi, Walkmans and video cameras. Now we're buying PCs (Sony VAIO), PDAs (Sony

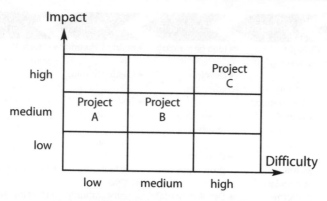

Figure 3.3 An innovation matrix

Clié) and mobile phones (Sony Ericsson). Yes, consumer electronics is big on innovation, but no one does it as consistently and as well as Sony.

So, what is the best number of product innovation projects to have in the matrix? This will obviously depend on your industry, where you are starting from, your strategic idea and a whole host of other factors. But there are some broad guidelines.

Over a three-year period, a successful business should be looking to achieve 50 per cent of sales from innovations – new products or services, or significant improvements on existing ones. To put it another way, 50 per cent of your sales should be from things you did not sell in their present form three years ago.

There is an unavoidable failure rate in innovation, so this should encourage you to look for the highest number of projects to hedge your bets. If you only have one project it has to succeed. On the other hand, the more projects you have, the less attention each one will get, which will increase the chances of failure and provide a greater number of excuses for it. Five to ten projects is probably a good number. And the more the project can be described as an outcome rather than a solution, the more chance you have of succeeding unexpectedly. Five projects with a clear but broad outcome are better than ten specific ideas. The 'Healthy eating for kids' project is better than the 'Tasty cereal bar for kids' project.

2. Funnels and charters

A lot of companies now use an 'innovation funnel' to describe the three key stages of the pre-launch innovation process – development, validation and refinement. The swirls in Figure 3.4 are my addition, to acknowledge that at each stage there need to be reiterations to get it right. At the start and end of the funnel and before entering each of the three stages there should be a review meeting and a formal buy-in to prepare the ground for the next stage, because of all the cost, money and effort that each step involves. The review should be given by the working team to the 'steering team', which would normally comprise the key decision makers from all the relevant functions in the business (very often, it is the board).

To encourage good discipline, the project should start with a charter which is revised for each subsequent stage. As the project progresses, the charter can become more detailed until the pre-launch stage, when the full business case is presented. However, you should still be able to summarise it on no more than two pages. Suggested headings for the charter are shown in Figure 3.5.

My strong advice is that a) charters should be pre-circulated and enough time should be allowed for a full discussion, and b) all members of the steering committee actually sign the charter at every stage. This makes it very clear that they have had their chance to ask questions, that they agree, and that they are committed and accept the risks involved. In my experience, very few businesses do this.

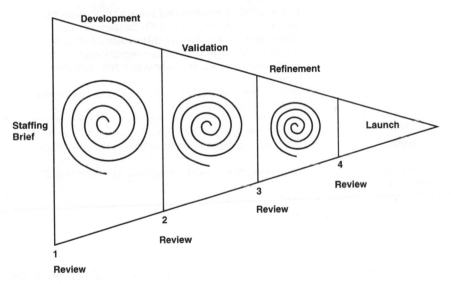

Figure 3.4 An innovation funnel

3. The ideas generator

The innovation process should really start with an ideas generator. This is a facilitated workshop-style meeting, which owes a big debt to Art Fry's Post-it note. In fact, the name 'ideas generator' refers to Added Value's particular way of running meetings, using Post-it notes and big felt tip pens. The Post-its allow people to scrawl down their ideas, swap them, display them, mix them up and juxtapose them. The pens are actually smelly pens – each colour has

The market opportunity	This summarises the opportunity identified in the market in three ways: Where is the growth going to come from (e.g. targeting a new consumer segment or improving a benefit in an existing segment)? How the business is going to address this (e.g. using an existing brand or new brand)? What will be the source of business (i.e. stealing share from competitors or category growth)?
The strategic rationale	What opportunity or problem for the brand or company does this address?
Summary of the key target for the opportunity	**Who are we trying to appeal to?** Description of the primary target audience including the size of market as well as demographic and attitudinal typologies. **Why will they choose this product?** Characterises the functional and emotional needs or benefits desired by consumers. **When will they choose this product?** Identifies the key occasions the product/service is consumed. **Where will they consume this product?** Identifies key consumption locations, or key geographies, or buying location i.e. the trade or channel that the product/service is bought. **What is the product?** Outlines the categories, products, brands and characteristics.
Action standard	What performance benchmark or hurdle has to be achieved or cleared in order to pass to the next stage?
Resources required	What resources – people, time, money – are needed?

Figure 3.5 Project charter

its own non-toxic fragrance – and we import them in caseloads from the United States. They're really a gimmick, but they do give people a small encouragement to lose their inhibitions and free up their thinking.

The aim of the first IG meeting (apart from dispensing with all those silly inhibitions) is to get a brief agreed and to make sure that all the relevant ideas are out on the table before things really gets going. The IG meetings should then continue regularly throughout the innovation process, and should involve as wide a range of people as possible: the working team, other key people in the company, partner agencies, experts in the field, opinion leaders, potential buyers, creative resources – whoever might have a contribution to make. The charter documents mentioned earlier are really just a summary of the IG's output.

To be effective, an IG needs a clear task and a trained, well briefed facilitator who is not part of the project team. You need to think carefully about who should be at the meeting. Avoid the political invitees and go for the people you really want: the people you think will work well together and will make a useful contribution. By all means have a few wild cards but make this a deliberate decision. And try to limit the group to ten people.

Obviously, you should agree the process with the facilitator but it's important that you let the facilitator do his or her job, which means the final decision on process should be his/hers. The facilitator should then brief every attendee before the meeting, explain the task and the rough process to be followed and, most importantly, should give people a chance to get any agendas or issues out in the open.

The choice of location for the meeting can make an enormous difference to the level of creativity and its eventual success. So choose a nice room with big windows that is three times the size normally needed for a group of ten. There should be lots of space to put up flip charts and good facilities. Also, make sure that you prepare the stimulus with care and creativity, guided by the facilitator. You want a series of short – 20 minute maximum – provocations, not lengthy boring presentations.

Apply the normal guidelines for creative meetings. People should be encouraged to:

- Listen generously.
- Build on ideas, don't censor (that comes later!).
- Make the point first and the justification afterwards.
- Express concerns and ask questions as 'How?' questions, such as 'Great idea. How could we make it easier to use?' Drop the people who insist on saying, 'Are you serious? That will never work because it is impossible to use.'

The value of using Post-it notes throughout the meeting is to encourage people to speak in headlines and get to the point. It also gives all individuals airtime as they present their thoughts and ideas and issues. With Post-its, you can build on ideas and regroup them as you make new connections, as well as allowing people to tune out from time to time, without losing the thread of the meeting.

At various points, you take the temperature with a simple voting system. 'OK. You've got five points to give. You can award them all to one idea or spread them out, it's up to you.' But be careful not to close the debate down or force people to take up positions they can't back down from.

The IG process will be effectively a diamond, building out from the task, getting people more and more outside their comfort zone and then bringing things to some kind of conclusion. At the end of the meeting you should always ask people for the one moment, piece of inspiration, idea, conclusion that they will remember the following day. These are what we call the 'Aha!'s.

A typical IG process would look like this.

Generator: sample process

THE TASK

To develop a new range of revolutionary ready to drink alcoholic beverages.

Time	Process	Desired output
9.00	**Introductions** Explanation of 'good behaviour'. Shape of the session.	Understanding of the generator process
9.10	**Warm-up** Ask everyone to introduce themselves and ask them, if you could have a free alcoholic beverage on tap at home forever, what would it be?	Break the ice, ensure everyone gets to know each other
9.20	**Task introduction** Client introduces the task and explains the reasons we're all here. Check for clarity.	Ensure everyone knows why we are here, what we're trying to achieve
9.40	**Brainbank** Spontaneous download of ideas. Capture on Post-it notes and share.	Spontaneous download of early solutions
10.30	**Break**	Review progress
10.45	**Creative exercise 1: consumer role play** Divide into pairs. Provide each pair with a role. Ask then to describe a big night out. What ideas does this stimulate?	Ideas, based on consumer behaviour/ insight
11.30	**Creative exercise 2: corporate takeover** Divide into threes. Allocate each a brand such as Sony or Mercedes. If that organisation took over your company, what would its drinks look and feel like?	Ideas from the perspective of new, non-alcoholic brands
12.15	**Creative exercise 3: colour** Divide into threes. Allocate each a colour. What does it stand for? What ideas does this stimulate?	Ideas from associations with different colours

Time	Process	Desired output
13.00	**Lunch**	
13.45	**Review selection** Each person to choose top 3–5 ideas. Group and theme into lead areas	Selection of 'big' ideas
14.30	**Quick break and energiser**	Maintain energy
14.45	**Solution building** Divide into teams. Work up lead themes into more detailed product ideas.	More detailed idea development
15.30	**Share and build** Take feedback from rest of team, continue to build.	Improved ideas
16.00	**Visualisation** Create mood boards/pack visuals.	Idea expressed through visual imagery
16.30	**Final presentation** 'Sell' your idea	"80%" solutions
16.50	**Personal highlights** 'Aha' moment. Individual actions.	End on a high
17.00	**Close**	Leave, tired but happy.

Figure 3.6 Sample Generator process

While to some this may sound like old hat, apple pie or motherhood, I defy you to name one meeting that actually followed all the guidelines. The most common mistakes or omissions are: poor team selection, no pre-briefing, poor definition of task, a facilitator who wasn't allowed to do his or her job or didn't really have one. And also don't forget the importance of a good venue and good stimulus.

Many years ago I was put in charge of an innovation team tasked by the main board director of Unilever in charge of detergents to come up with some really ground-breaking ideas. Not a very clear brief, no clue as to how we should define the market, what the overall strategy was (it was never clear he had one to be fair), but never mind. It was a great team comprising some really bright marketers and technical people, we had carte blanche on what we did and a seemingly limitless budget. We came up with some great ideas – none were ever launched but that is another story. At the start of the project, I looked up the output of several other previous innovation teams. Every one had come up with the idea of a product to clean carpets and curtains, something Unilever did not and still doesn't make. It suddenly

struck me why they had all had this idea. The meetings were held in the typical hotel conference room where the two dominant pieces of stimulus are
curtains and carpets. Procter did eventually launch Febreze – it came from a
technical insight I believe.

And finally, don't forget that it is the 'Whynotters' who move companies.
If you let them flourish, great output is guaranteed.

Whynotters move companies

The next time you're in a meeting, look around and identify the
yesbutters, the notnowers and the whynotters.
God bless the whynotters. They dare to dream. And to act. By acting,
they achieve what others see as unachievable.
Why not, indeed?
Before the yesbutters yesbut you right out of business.

---

4. The role of research and the power of the prototype

Most potential innovation is killed by research. This point cannot be over-
stressed. Right up until the preparation of the business case (at which point
you do need evaluation and numbers), the innovation process is one of learning and insight gathering, so many of the points about the dangers of research
that were made in the Insight section are just as relevant here. Throughout the
development and refinement stages of the process, the whole team has
constantly to be reminded:

It does not matter what they liked or disliked, what did we learn?

One very large consumer goods business still to this day runs 'Inno-checks' at
the start of the process in the hope of screening out the obvious losers. Not
surprisingly they still develop an alarming number of faster horses rather than
motor cars.

To keep this simple, for everything up to the evaluation stage (which is
right at the end), let's just focus on five things:

- Concentrate on talking to opinion leaders, articulate and creative people
  who have some interest and knowledge about the category.
- Use quantitative surveys to check facts and test assumptions or prototypes, but not ideas.
- Always write concepts in this way – insight, proposition, reason to

believe. For example: 'Sushi provides a great alternative to fast food at lunchtime. It's tasty and very healthy – perhaps it's one reason why most Japanese live much longer than the average American or European.' In this way you can really understand and learn from how the concept is working: what is interesting, what is credible, what is insightful.

- Don't rely on concepts unless you have to. Wherever possible, and as soon as possible, use actual prototypes. The only exception to this is in financial services which is, after all, a promise written on a piece of paper. But use prototypes for every other category. And please don't ask me to imagine a fizzy drink that tastes better than Coke but is better for me than orange juice – I can't, but I might if I tried it.
- Never ignore research findings, always learn from them, but trust your own judgement more than the 'consumers'.

When it comes to evaluation there is a large, profitable and very professional industry that can do this for you. The firms all have their own proprietary tools with names like 'Evaluator' or 'Micro Market test' – or perhaps even 'the Terminator'. The good ones evaluate ideas and provide volume estimates, as you should, based on the following five criteria:

- Is it unique?
- Is it credible?
- Is it relevant?
- Would you buy it and how often?
- How much would you pay for it?

Every good technique then applies two factors to aim off for the facts that a) not everyone is going to hear about this because you will not achieve the impact you hope, and b) you cannot entirely trust what people say in research.

To build on the last point and provide a useful rule of thumb, focus on the 'top box score'. The fourth of the criteria above, 'Would you buy it?', is of course the most important when it comes to evaluation, and the 'respondent' (person in the research) is normally asked to agree with one of five statements: Would definitely buy, Would probably buy, Don't know, Would probably not buy, Would definitely not buy. Often the result is shown as an average, but you should always look at the top box, Would definitely buy. The minimum you need to believe that the idea has potential is 25 per cent, and 50 per cent is a winner even if the bottom box is also 50 per cent (which would give you an average score of only 2.5). The point is that you should be looking for the exceptional and not the average.

A final reflection on the role of research illustrates a number of points, but especially the point about prototypes. Imagine that you're researching into a new type of brake. It goes off and comes on many times a second, but without the driver knowing, to avoid the wheels locking up and the car going into a skid. A concept insight that was 'Most people are unhappy with their brakes' would get less response than 'Most people worry that their car will skid if they jam on the brakes.' The insight is important, but however sharp the insight, it is likely that most people would reject the idea of brakes that go on and come off, and instead stick with brakes that come on and stay on, thank you very much for asking. But no one who has ever had a car with ABS brakes would willingly go back to one that does not. They are now fitted as standard on most cars, but for a long time they were a desirable extra that people would happily pay a premium for. As a concept, though, they would never have made it through most innovation research.

5. Staying on track and managing the team

This section has provided one view of an innovation process, which has been used successfully many times. However, the most important thing is that there should be some kind of structure for decision making as an innovation progresses towards launch. It is not so important what process you use, just that you have one and that everyone understands it and their role in it.

Apparently, there is a large cosmetics business which gets country marketing teams to develop an innovation (a relaunch of an existing brand or a new brand) all the way through to the final mix – pack, product, pricing, advertising. It is then presented, together with the research results, to a senior panel who listen to the case and give the thumbs up, or down. It seems an expensive way to go about things compared with the funnel approach which provides checks along the way, but you can see how this could work very well. The country teams make very sure their mix is in great shape before the final presentation, so a concrete, tangible idea is presented, not one where you have to use your imagination, and then the most experienced team in the business gives its verdict. Overall, the business may find that less money is wasted in this way than through all the hidden costs – in both time and money – of the more staged process.

Process, as long as it is clear and understood, is not the critical factor. Nor is the idea necessarily critical – there are lots of good ideas and you will never know which was 'the best'. The difference between success and failure in innovation lies in:

- the quality and motivation of the team
- their ability to address conflict and overcome failure
- the subsequent implementation.

The implementation – or impact – is dealt with in the next stage of the Five I's process. For now, let's focus on keeping the team on track.

For many years Added Value has made use of a team-building technique developed by Beechwood called 'The Mat'. The Mat is a journey you have to make across squares, moving like a king does in chess. Some squares bleep and if you hit one, you have to turn back, retrace your steps exactly and start again. The team is divided into the walkers and the guiders, and they are given five minutes together to agree a process (in effect, a strategy) to get the walkers across as quickly as possible. Once they start, they are not allowed to speak, so all communication must be by hand signals. The guiders have to work out how to remember which squares bleep and how to pass this information on to the walkers quickly and effectively – particularly since this is a timed exercise. They are given three goes – the successful route changes each time – and the time taken to complete the task, to 'win', falls typically from 15 minutes in the first run to as low as 3 minutes in the last run. The reason for this is that by the last run they have learnt the following, and learnt it the hard way:

- how to work as a team with clear roles, responsibilities and accountability
- how to get everyone involved with passion for the outcome
- how to make decisions that are clear and accepted by the whole group
- how to overcome conflict and cope with failure – and learn from both
- the need for leadership and the leader's need to listen and make balanced decisions, using all the resources of the group.

There is normally one breakthrough moment when, in the review session between runs, someone suggests it might be a good idea to ask the walkers what help and signals make it easier for them. Another is when someone points out that, having hit a very frustrating bleep just near the finishing post, the team must not switch off but must stay focused in order to guide the walkers back to the start without incurring any penalties by 'bleeping' on the way back. In other words they learn that failure is inevitable, that it is impossible to stay on plan the whole time, and that success depends as much on how you cope with this as how you create the passion to succeed.

In summary, they learn all the lessons of successful teams. This 'game' takes no more than an hour and a half to run and every innovation team should be required to go through it – or whatever other team-building game you prefer – at the start of the project and ideally once or twice during the life of the project. I have participated in The Mat ten or more times, and have run the exercise at least as often, and I learn or relearn something every time.

If there is just one thing The Mat teaches you, and one thing that a success-ful innovation team has to cope with, it is this issue of failure. With the most divine irony, after writing the last paragraph, I took a break to watch England get knocked out of the World Cup by Brazil – it is 9.30 a.m. on 21 June 2002. The looks on the players' faces, the expressions of the fans and poor old David Seaman, who knows he let in a soft goal, make this point about failure so vividly. How do you pick yourself up from a disappointment like that and prepare to win in Germany in 2006?

Winning the World Cup is of course far more important than developing a winning innovation, and at least with a failure in innovation you do not neces-sarily have to wait four years to try again. But there are parallels, what Synec-tics call the 'dark night of the innovator': the bad research result, the prototype that doesn't work, the moment when the steering committee turns you down. In every successful story of innovation there are several such moments. If you have not done your groundwork – designed a process, got the whole team committed to the process and the goal, confronted in advance how you are going to work as a team – you are left with only one hope. Perhaps that's just the idea that there is an Art Fry somewhere in your organisation who will be an innovator and do it all himself.

The innovation process recommended earlier took the form of a funnel, but in fact innovation can also be pictured as a wonky Christmas tree. When the brief is first written, the process of innovation is seen as a straight purposeful route towards the star that is the new product at the end of the process. Starting from a wide, inclusive base, the innovation process narrows as the non-starters and false leads are winnowed out. There is then a reiteration of the brief based on progress made, which widens out the process to include new ideas and fresh thinking. This in turn is narrowed

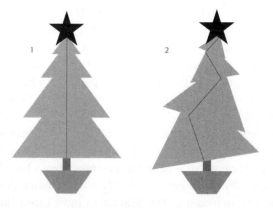

Figure 3.7 Innovation as a Christmas tree

down to a point where a further reiteration is necessary, and so on. If only innovation were as simple and methodical as that. The truth is that while the process may bear some resemblance to the one just described, the Christmas tree nearly always goes wonky as the aims of the project and the thinking behind the brief start to shift. There is still a star at the top of the tree, but you often find it in a completely different place from the one you expected at the start of the process. Which reminds us of Christopher Columbus, all over again.

WINNING INNOVATION

In order to emphasise the importance of the innovation process and the role of the team, the value of a great idea has been somewhat downplayed in this chapter. But, of course, the process needs a great idea – that's what provides the passion to drive the team on, because you are all impatient to get it onto the market.

The source of winning strategic ideas, which end up in winning innovations, was covered in the last section, but to build on this and the sources of insight, here are some more places to look for great ideas:

The technical team

If you lift the constraints you normally put on your technical team, in particular cost and price, what great ideas do they have knocking around? If you asked a furniture maker how you could give people good quality furniture at low prices, he would tell you, get them to make the furniture themselves. Ikea has built a great business out of this.

Abroad

What products are on the market elsewhere in the world? People are not that different around the world, and if a few million people like a product in some other country, the chances are the people in your country will too. Fromage frais in France, Guinness in Ireland, rap music in the United States, sushi in Japan – all of these were evidently popular in their domestic markets but very odd to the rest of us at some point. Everyone talks about the Internet as some kind of discontinuity, but France had a version of this, Minitel, for years. In fact, the experience of Minitel could have been used to predict many things about how the Internet would be used: the importance of giving it low or no cost to encourage take-up, for example.

The periphery of the market

For any market, look at what people with lots of time, money or expertise are using and then figure out how to adapt it for the mainstream. This has been the basis of mainstream innovation ideas like SLR cameras, personal banking, utility vehicles, personal computers: the list is endless.

Bloody-mindedness

This has already been described as challenging market assumptions, but let's take it one stage further to sheer bloody-mindedness. Swiss watches are expensive with crafted mechanical movements, Japanese watches are cheap with quartz movements. That was the accepted wisdom before the bloody-mindedness of Swatch.

Theft

Some of the best ideas are stolen from other markets. Supermarkets stole the idea of loyalty cards from airlines. The beer companies stole the idea of a 'Lite' version from cigarette companies, who probably stole it from somewhere else. Keep your eyes and ears open and steal with pride.

History

Try re-presenting past successes to a younger audience – Smirnoff Ice and Bacardi Breezer are cocktails similar to the cocktails that our grandparents liked.

Go premium or go adequate

There is always room for a better, more expensive version. Häagen Dazs proved this in spades in the ice-cream market. There is also often room for a stripped down version that just about meets the need but at a fraction of the price. SouthWest Airlines pioneered this into a whole new category which took the airline industry by storm and was successfully copied by Easyjet in Europe.

Attack yourself

If you stop to think about it, no-one knows better than you, how to beat your-self. Jack Welch professes to be a an advocate of this philosophy, the idea that you should always aim to make yourself obsolete. Work out how you would enter your own market and attack yourself, then work out whether you can pre-empt this. Be your own competition. Microsoft have taken this to a whole new level, as their internal rivalries are far more effective and challenging than the ones provided by their competition.

Very occasionally, innovation is so dramatic and so new that it is hard to put your finger on its source. As Art Fry found, there are some ideas that are too original to put into words. These kind of ideas are often called 'Discontinuities'. There was an excellent article by Bower and Christensen in the *Harvard Business Review* (January 1995) called 'Disruptive technologies, catching the wave'[5] in which they cited the personal computer as an example of a disruptive technology, or a discontinuity in the market. Certainly, the emergence of the PC cut across the direction in which the market seemed to be heading, which was then driven by IBM's mainframe computers. Bower and Christensen make some valuable points about how to spot such a discontinuity, pointing out that you will not find them by researching your current buyers, because discontinuities normally germinate in an adjacent market and grow from there to attack your core business. PCs found their initial audience among writers, college professors and designers rather than the big corporates. If you had researched the big corporates, as IBM surely did, they would have fed back a lot of reassuring things about the negatives of PCs as they were then – too slow, not enough memory and not enough security. (Remember this was before the Internet had democratised knowledge, and in many companies a certain level of seniority was required before you gained access to the precious mainframe.)

PCs came, found an audience that had different attitudes and priorities, and over time they improved and closed the gap in terms of speed and power. In what must have felt like no more than an instant, there were suddenly mainstream rivals pouring out of left field to challenge the Big Blue. This was compounded by IBM's decision that software was not a core business – a costly 'blink' that opened the door for Microsoft. The result was that one of the greatest businesses in the world was almost brought to its knees. Credit to IBM, it has now caught the Internet wave and regained its stride.

I was fascinated by this article. How do you spot discontinuities? How do you create them? It confirmed my view that mainstream research is not the best place to find great insight for strategy and innovation.

Shortly after reading the article I was eavesdropping on a conversation between my 10-year-old daughter and her 17-year-old female cousin. 'What's it like to be a teenager?' my daughter asked, very seriously. I listened as her cousin gave a very considered response. Yes, you got more freedom but there were also extra responsibilities and worries, about exams, boyfriends and how you look. My daughter could only think in terms of extensions of her life as it was, staying up a bit later, more exams and so on, because between her and being a teenager lay our human discontinuity, puberty. Then it struck me. I had known her cousin, my niece, since she was a small child, and while she was undoubtedly different now, I could still recognise the same child with all her characteristics and personality in the older teenager. Discontinuities only ever look discontinuous when you look forward. When you look back they are evolutionary, and you can recognise all the factors that came together to cause the evolutionary change.

All the information IBM needed to counter the PC threat was available to it. It knew all about the technology, and had it made the connection, it also knew how business and the world was changing, from an era of rank and structure to one of freedom of information and connectivity. What it lacked was the alchemy necessary to pull it together, and the goal embedded in a clear strategy to give it the incentive. Instead what it had was what every large organisation has – inertia, a pattern of how it saw the world and, of course, a vested interest.

To change that requires the Five 'I's process – follow it and it works. Well, it will if the world ever gets to see the result of all this wonderful insight, ideas and innovation – and for that, we need to find out how to create – impact!

THE STUFF THAT GETS IN THE WAY OF INNOVATION

1. Trying to do too much and lack of new competencies

Most businesses try to do too many things. This could be because of over-ambition, poor management, hedging their bets, or a strange habit of letting projects die slowly through natural causes rather than killing them off to make room for others. You can hedge your bets by keeping a number of projects running, and it is true that most innovation fails. But it is truer that the more you do, the more you give yourself the excuse to fail, and most innovation fails through poor implementation rather than it being a poor idea.

For the few that remain, there must be an acceptance of the need for new competencies and an appetite for the means to obtain them. If the innovation is balanced across the near-in and far-out, the comfortable and the scary, and it should be, then somewhere along the line the business will need some new competencies. 'We are going to leverage the (product) brand into our own retail outlet.' 'Great, but does anyone know how to run a shop?' The good entrepreneur is much more alert to the need to acquire new competencies than the brilliance and uniqueness of the innovation. By limiting the innovations, the business can free up the resources to go looking for the new competency.

2. No brief

Most innovation projects have very poor briefs if any brief at all. Innovation, the word and the pursuit, became very fashionable in the late 1980s and 1990s. One chairman of a very large FMCG business went very public with his top three priorities – innovation, innovation and innovation. As I was working with his operating companies at the time I can tell you they did not have a clue about why this was so important or what constituted good innovation. A lot of brands were messed around and fragmented unnecessarily and unprofitably as a result. As I said at the beginning of the chapter, innovation needs a written brief and a stable, committed team.

3. Easier to say no and no incentives

So it's always better to say no! This simple matrix (Figure 3.8) illustrates a very pernicious cause of poor or no innovation. The scores relate the marks out of 10 you get from the organisation (plaudits, promotion, bonus) for saying yes or no, and for good outcomes or bad outcomes. The scores were supplied by a real team of managers in a

If you say yes ...	... and it works	... and it fails	Points available
Score	7	0	7
If you say no ...	...and it works	... and it fails	Points available
Score	4	6	10

Figure 3.8 When someone proposes a new idea ...

business that was driving for innovation. Even if you say yes and it works, you only get 7 because success has many fathers, and you get no points for failure (one person wanted to put a minus score). If you say no and it would have worked (for example, the competition does it successfully) you don't score lower than 4 because the circumstances were never the same and you can cover your tracks. Conversely you score a 6 for being an 'I told you so' in the event that the competition do it and it fails. Add the scores up, as in game theory, and it is always better to say no. This is what it feels like to work in a business with layers of bureaucracy all able to say no and very poor incentives for taking the kind of personal risks necessary to bring an innovation to market successfully.

4. No prototypes

'Imagine what it would be like if ...' Well, most people can't. Spend less on research and more on experimentation using prototypes. Bake the cake, build the store (even if only 'virtually' on computer), write the software – make it real.

5. Lack of senior sponsorship

More than just the steering team who pitch up for the innovation review, the senior team need to be involved. There need to be unofficial channels where the working team can talk off-line, cry on shoulders and get help to clear blockages. The best innovation projects I have worked on were those that had the regular and committed involvement of senior people. If senior people spent less time interfering in advertising and more time getting involved with innovation – other than just screaming for it – there would be better ads and better innovation.

CHAPTER 4

Impact

Impact. The word suggests a moment. A sliver of time so fine that it can only be captured by the fastest shutter speed. The beads of sweat flying off a boxer's face as he takes an upper-cut on the chin ... the bowed strings of a racquet as they flatten a tennis ball at the moment of contact ... or the sublime atomic violence of a demolition ball as it swings into the corner of an unloved tower block.

But if you speak about moments like these to a boxer, a tennis player, a demolition man or even a photographer, they'll have nothing to tell you about impact. For them, the moment of impact is useful only as a way of distinguishing a period of meticulous preparation from its expected (and, hopefully, successful) result. In fact, good coaches of ball games rarely make reference to 'impact'; instead, they focus on back-lift and follow-through. If both of those are right, the desired impact is guaranteed.

As in tennis (oh yes, and boxing and demolition), so in marketing. If the first three 'I's are right, the fifth 'I' – investment return – is guaranteed. Well, that's nearly true. Marketing differs from other disciplines in that its 'impact' is rather more squashy and harder to freeze-frame. And for that reason it certainly benefits from a bit of a careful examination.

There is no one 'I' in the Five 'I's process that is more or less important than any other – each one is critical to the overall goal of profitable growth. But without impact, there is no point. This is the stage in the process when the outside world – and the rest of the organisation – actually get to see something, so it had better be the right something that they see.

For a lot of the marketing world, impact is all about ads, and for a lot of the advertising world, ads mean little bits of Hollywood or TV commercials, which affect the way people feel about brands. Far too often the intended compliment, 'They do great marketing' translates as 'I like their ads'.

But advertising is only a part of the picture – and it's becoming a less important part as time goes on. Life used to be so simple. You took some notional percentage of the revenue of the brand (or future revenue if it was a new brand) – 5 per cent is a good round number – and you invested 60 per cent above the line and 40 per cent below the line. 'Above the line' meant advertising – TV, cinema, radio, press or posters – and 'below the line' meant

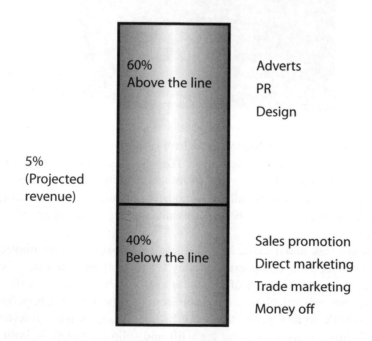

Figure 4.2 Revenue brands

promotions – sampling, money-off, free gifts or competitions. Half your money was wasted, but you didn't know which half, but that was OK because it meant the other half was working.

But today when we talk about impact, we mean every single point at which a brand impacts on the rest of the world – from a sponsored sports event, to a conversation overheard on a bus, to a logo on a blimp high above our heads. In considering impact, we shouldn't forget the importance of impact within a company, but the real focus of this chapter is getting a bigger 'bang for your buck', externally. (The more formal term for 'bang for your buck' is ROMI, or return on marketing investment, but we'll come to that later.)

Impact and, by implication branding, is all about fame. We're told that as a society we are obsessed with celebrity, which of course is true. You can be famous for 15 minutes, like a quiz show winner; you can be famous for being infamous like Jack the Ripper; and some people like Tara Palmer-Tomkinson even manage to be famous just for being famous. But with brands, we're seeking the kind of fame that is much harder to earn – a durable fame based on a specific and positive competitive advantage. Celebrities who have this kind of fame are the people who have actually done something that is worthwhile and out of the ordinary. The brands that enjoy this kind of fame are the ones you want to buy because they offer a clear positive benefit that none of their competitors do.

As master marketer Jeremy Bullmore has pointed out, one of the curious things about fame is that it is 'spectacularly untargeted'. He writes, 'Most famous people are known to an infinitely greater number of people than their particular talent or profession would seem to demand or deserve.' In marketing terms, this means that we must be prepared to spread our brand's fame far beyond the immediate market of potential customers.

To create this impact we have to engage our audience, and in order to do that we must first understand them and then create a connection between our actions and words, and their interests and passions. Film makers are endlessly reminded to show and not to tell. We don't just want to be told how wicked Dr Hannibal Lecter is, we want to see his unspeakable villainy with our own eyes. The same applies to marketing. How our brand behaves is far more important than what we assert about it. Of course, what we tell people provides the context for our brand's behaviour to be interpreted correctly. But it's not enough to be told that something is 'simply the best', however many times that message is repeated. Actions speak louder than words.

This principle underpins many of the great ads of the past: the Ford Cortina glued to a poster with Araldite, above the slogan 'It also sticks handles to teapots'. Even the product comparisons that prove that one detergent washes whiter than another are a variation on the 'show, don't tell' theme. But as was said earlier, advertising – even advertising that shows rather than tells – is still only one element of true impact.

Impact is 360 degrees. It requires us to use every technique, every medium and every aspect of our brand to connect and create a reaction. We can no longer rely on commercial TV to beam our brand into the nation's homes on a nightly basis. Patterns of media consumption are changing, for a whole host of reasons: the proliferation of channels, the use of video and DVD and competition from the Internet, to name but three. There are now even technologies like the TiVo which (horror of horrors) allow viewers to edit out advertising altogether, while watching (virtually) live TV.

Nigel Bogle, a founder of the agency, Bartle Bogle Hegarty – and one of the best admen around – believes that we are leaving behind a whole era of communication and marketing. In a recent article, he contrasted what he calls the 'interrupt and repeat' model of advertising to the new approach to brand impact which is currently emerging.

> *The most important thing for us all to grasp as marketers is that we have ended one era of communication, which I call the interrupt-and-repeat model, and we are moving into another. For the last 50 years, what we have done through commercial television is interrupt programming and repeat a message. That message did not have to be interesting – we could just go out and repeat our message four or five times and it was drilled into our memories. There are lots of slogans and jingles that have not run for years, but which we can remember because we used repetition.*
>
> *But repetition is no longer part of our armoury in the way it was before, because people are editing stuff out now. We have become a society of editors, and that is why fame is on the agenda in this discussion. As marketers, we now have to engage consumers. Everything is content now, whether you are a brand or a programme.*
>
> *If you are a brand, your competition is life and not simply other brands. That means that advertising agencies and marketers have got to look differently at the way they promote themselves. They have got to ask just how interesting their brand is and how they are going to engage attention.*[6]

'Engaging attention' is a far broader and more challenging brief than simply 'advertising a product'. It requires us to think long and hard about how we approach our audience. We need to decide what kind of impact we want, and only then to start thinking about which channels can best deliver it. In marketing services jargon, this is 'a channel-neutral approach', and it should be based on a clear-eyed evaluation of the options rather than a knee-jerk resort to TV ads or posters, just because that's the way it's always been done before. Put another way, it means that you cannot delegate the task of impact to one executional agency unless that agency is expert in, and unbiased about, all the possible solutions to the brief. Trust me, none of them are.

Nike is already putting this into practice, if its 2002 campaign was anything to go by. The focus of its teen-targeted campaign was not 'a cool ad' but something it called Scorpion Football. This was a live event on a massive scale, held at the Millennium Dome in East London. You may have seen Premiership goal scorers running to the cameras lifting their shirts to reveal a black and white scorpion motif. You may have seen unbranded Adshells announcing 'You are now entering Fat Tail territory' with a picture of a nasty looking scorpion. But if you didn't see any of these, then don't be surprised – you weren't the target. Teens, however, saw, heard, discussed, logged on and were part of the whole Scorpion Football experience. Nike created a buzz – driving involvement in its brand for teens, not just an 'interrupt and repeat' message.

Certainly, if we do succeed in engaging attention in the right way, the results can be spectacular. Indeed, when things really start to happen for a brand, you can often see a multiplier effect occur, in which the impact produced is far greater than the sum of the individual parts. This multiplier could also be described as pushing people over a 'tipping point' from awareness into action. We could perhaps see it in terms of a mathematical formula:

$$I = f(n \times m \times p)t$$

Here, I = impact leading to action (not just impact that makes an impression); n = the number of times; m = the message or some aspect of the message; p = places or people; t = time. This could be expressed in plain English as: 'Impact that really makes you do something is a function of the number of times you hear the same thing from different people or in different places, over time.'

Let's take a simple example of impact leading to action. Imagine that you see a poster for a new film as you walk to the station one morning. On the train, you read a review in the paper. The following day you watch TV and see an interview with one of the actors talking about her role in the film. You go to a bar on Friday and overhear two people talking about the film and how much they enjoyed it. The result of this is that on Saturday you go and see the film. No one thing in itself would necessarily have made you go and see the film, but the cumulative effect of all these things makes it unmissable.

The same formula holds true for impact within an organisation. In most companies there is a good deal of cynicism about internal communication, and given the sheer number of internal initiatives, mission statements and change programmes, much of this cynicism is justified. All the more reason, then, to ensure that your message cuts through those negative emotions with the maximum impact. One way of doing this is to add an additional factor to the equation above: 'b' for bonus. Some kind of personal incentive related to a message is a remarkably powerful way of engaging internal attention.

Again, an example of this. After 20 years of constant cost-cutting and an obsession with bottom-line profit, your chairman wakes up one morning and announces that the route to success is to innovate in the area of customer service. By the time you've been to a conference, received a follow-up line management briefing, seen the posters in the canteen, attended the training course and overheard the chairman's chauffeur discussing the old man's latest enthusiasm in the car park, you'll probably have a hazy idea that something is afoot. But the penny really drops when you see a colleague get a promotion and pay rise for achieving a significant improvement in customer satisfaction scores. That's the moment when you finally get the message – and start coming up with a few ideas to put a smile back on those customers' faces.

A few years ago, Unilever decided to overhaul its whole approach to developing brand communications. It was a very comprehensive exercise led by a team of experienced senior managers, which Added Value supported in its own modest way. Not only did Unilever itself have a lot of best practice documents (it is, after all, one of the biggest, if not the biggest, investor in brands in the world), but it also leant on all its ad agencies – and agencies that aspired to work with the company – to contribute their best material and case studies. The output was turned into a series of manuals, and the new approach was communicated to 2,500 of Unilever's own marketing people and 1,500 people in its partner agencies. At the outset of the project, a survey was undertaken of how brand communications were developed, which included an audit of how briefs were delivered and how the implementation was managed, as well as who was involved, what disciplines were used and so on.

Unilever called its guide *Advanced Brand Communications*, or *ABC*, as it's more commonly known. There are three main stages in *ABC*. The first is what is called 'Inputs', which are effectively the first three 'I's of the Five 'I's process – insight, ideas and innovation. This stage concludes with an agreed brand positioning and a decision about what 'news' needs to be communicated. The second stage is the communications plan, and the third is the development of the creative content of that plan.

ABC places a lot of emphasis on the importance of the team in the process of creating impact. It insists there should be a team leader, defined roles and clear goals. As was the case with the innovation process, the precise nature of the process employed is less important than the fact that people's roles and responsibilities are clear and that there is a system for resolving conflict.

Perhaps more controversially, Unilever's new approach also stated that the means of communicating and connecting should be decided before the brief for the creative content was written. In other words, the company requires its marketing teams, including the partner agencies, to come up with a plan for how to connect the idea and innovation to the media and the channels of communication, before briefing the creative team. This may sound straight-forward, but it is in fact a radical departure from what Unilever did before and what most big advertisers still do. It is also at odds with the way that most ad agencies work.

Most agencies come up with a big idea, often for a TV ad, and only then do they start thinking about how to translate this to other kinds of advertis-ing and other types of promotion, like sales promotions, events, sponsor-ship, direct marketing or PR. Unfortunately, so dominant is the old 60/40 'above and below the line' model, that very little thought is given to the communications plan before the brief. Agencies, of course, will bristle at this and protest how budget, solution and channel-neutral they are; but they aren't, not in my experience, anyway. To achieve the best results, both the way that you connect and the way that you create content should be iterative processes, and they should run in tandem in an integrated way. Of course, it helps to have something to glue the whole plan together, so if you have a big idea at the very start, so much the better. But the creative briefs for specific activities and channels should certainly not be written until you have the overall framework.

Perhaps the general message of Unilever's *ABC* is that impact requires a thoughtful plan and a systematic process. In the past, fuzzy notions of intu-ition, creativity and serendipity were often over-emphasised in the process of creating impact. These factors may well have a part to play, but they may also be the reason 50 per cent of marketing expenditure is traditionally money down the pan. So in the rest of this chapter we're going to look at the plan and the process, in an attempt to create the most impact, to maximise the conver-sion from impact to action and from action to profitable growth. As always, there are five key areas:

1. Setting the budget
2. Building a 360 degree impact plan
3. Episodic marketing
4. Briefing and developing creative
5. Internal communications.

1. SETTING THE BUDGET – HOW MUCH IS ENOUGH?

The process of creating impact must start with setting a budget, but in theory there need be no limit on it. The limit on the budget depends on the financial returns and the degree of certainty that these returns will be achieved. Marketers are very fond of casting themselves in the role of long term visionaries and their financial colleagues as short term penny-pinchers, but this is not the case. Finance directors, just like the rest of us, report ultimately to the market and to the shareholders. A quick glance down the list of company valuations would demonstrate that investors have no problem investing for the long term and no problem taking risks. Anyone who thinks investors are a cautious breed should re-read economic history – from tulip mania to the dot.com bubble. However, there are two simple trade-offs for investors. There is a trade-off between time and return – 'I don't mind waiting but it better be worth it.' And there is a trade-off between certainty and returns – 'I'll take low risk but sure returns or risky but high returns, but I won't take risky and low.'

Marketers often have a lack of understanding of how to make a financial investment case, for example, by not knowing what a DCF yield means or not understanding the value of free cash in a business. This is understandable and easily rectified. The harder and less forgivable problem is marketers' inability to prove the returns or timescales involved in marketing investment. After almost 50 years of marketing experts in business, the best we can say is that half the money is wasted and that marketing investment has a long term effect but we don't know how long term. So the normal approach is to take last year's budget and add a bit, or to look at similar situations and deduce some pattern of investment expressed as a percentage of revenues.

This will be explored in more detail in the next stage of the Five 'I's process, but sadly I cannot promise to answer the fundamental questions. I can only offer some advice and approaches to close the gap between marketers' enthusiasm to spend and investors' need to understand the returns.

But let's not allow the best to be the enemy of the good. We can still do a lot better than 'last year's budget plus a bit' or 'what we spent last time'. When setting a budget, you should take a top-down, bottom-up, top-down approach, and look at it in the context of a minimum of two years and ideally five.

There is always scope for ambition in budget setting. And of course, the board believe you when you tell them you're going to change the rules, create a whole new category and generate riches beyond their wildest dreams. But all the ambition in the world is just a pipe dream unless you can produce a set of five-year revenues and margins that you think you can deliver. Oh yes, and you'll also need a great impact plan. And, the deal needs

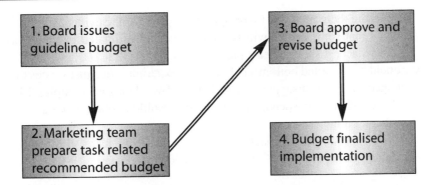

Figure 4.3 Budget plus

to be that if you miss it by more than 10 per cent, they will kill your children. This normally gets some sense into the debate and allows the senior team to review a reasonable plan and give a view on the likely budget you are going to work with.

You can now proceed to the next stage and develop a plan from the bottom up. This should start with how you are going to connect, then define what deliverables are required from each activity, and say how much this will cost. From this, you can work back up to a total budget. And here you are helped enormously by taking a perspective of more than a year. This means that you won't cram all the money into the first year when the corporate enthusiasm is high and you are the number one priority, in the expectation that in year two the slightest problem anywhere else in the business will mean the budget will get cut. The deal with the senior team should be that, at least for two years, if you deliver the plan, you keep your budget – or you will kill their children.

With this implied threat, the senior team can do the last top-down exercise. They should start by looking at any variance with the first plan you presented and decide whether the arguments put forward seem reasonable. To help with this, there are five questions they can ask:

- What evidence do you have that this is the right amount of money to achieve these specific tasks?
- What evidence do you have for the returns for each activity?
- Why this mix – why not more on x and less on y or vice versa?
- If we took away $500k where would you make the cut?
- If we gave you another $500k where you would invest it?

These last two questions are very effective (incidentally, they work when reviewing any proposal from an external supplier) because they reveal instantly where there might be fat or opportunity. As for the evidence, it has to be accepted that some of this will be qualitative and estimated in some way, but give it your best shot. At least prepare the answers.

We could have started bottom-up, but in my experience this just wastes time and sets people up for disappointment. Personally, when I go shopping I like some idea of what I can spend, even if the irresistible bargain may cause me to change my budget.

This is a very simple approach but it works. So if we have an initial top-down budget, pass go, collect $200 and proceed to the plan.

2. BUILDING A 360 DEGREE IMPACT PLAN

What follows is a way of developing a 360 degree communications plan that starts with the brand objectives and the specific tasks that come out of these objectives. We then look at the way the brand could connect with people's lives using every possible channel, medium and mechanism at our disposal. Next, we form a plan based on cost effectiveness, and we end with the briefs for both the creative and the channels/media buyers. It does not yet cover the idea of doing all of this 'episodically', that comes next.

The plan is logical, sensible and creative – but it is also a little theoretical. To my certain knowledge no one has ever actually done this in precisely the way set out and with quite the rigour implied. But versions of it have been done many times, and have produced much more imaginative and effective communications plans than the typical 'media plan', which is really the old 60/40 model, made to look comprehensive, when in fact it's just plain dull (Figure 4.4). See what I mean?

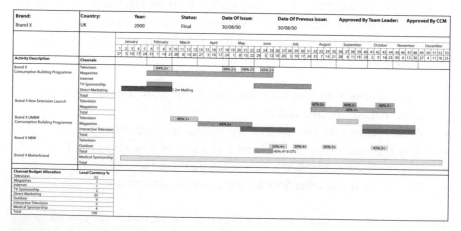

Figure 4.4 A typical communication plan

We can definitely improve on this. My confidence in the method proposed is based on its originators. In 1999 Added Value merged (well, we thought it was a merger) with an independent media buying agency, CIA. Eventually the new group was itself bought by WPP, and new possibilities have opened up, but during the two-year 'marriage' of Added Value and CIA, we focused on combining brand and insight expertise with media and channel experts to develop the best communication planning process. The process has been used successfully with clients such as Singapore Airlines and Mercedes, but as noted, although the basic principles were applied, it was not implemented in precisely the way it was originally conceived. So perhaps the approach can stand a little compression, short cuts and adaptation, but to let you make up your own mind, here is the all-singing, all-dancing version. And, no surprises – once again, it's a five-stage process (Figure 4.5).

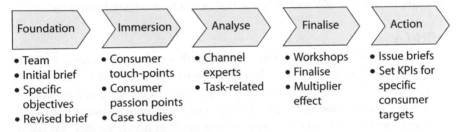

Foundation	Immersion	Analyse	Finalise	Action
• Team • Initial brief • Specific objectives • Revised brief	• Consumer touch-points • Consumer passion points • Case studies	• Channel experts • Task-related	• Workshops • Finalise • Multiplier effect	• Issue briefs • Set KPIs for specific consumer targets

Figure 4.5 The five-stage process

Stage 1: Foundation

Your starting point will be the brand positioning, and as part of the brand positioning tool kit, the definition shifts from where the brand is to where you want it to be. If the communications plan is for the launch of a new brand or brand extension, there will be the 'who? what? why? when? where?' of the new product to work with.

The first step is to form the team and run through the process with them, so everyone is clear how it works and what they are supposed to contribute. Who should be in the team? Basically, a mixture of the brand marketers, insight experts, creative agencies and media agencies. The leader of the team is the one who is responsible for setting the initial brief and selling the output up the line.

The team's first job is to interrogate the initial brief that comes from the brand positioning or innovation project and revise it to be as specific a set of communication tasks as possible. Remember, we don't just want to change the way people think; we want to affect their behaviour.

The specific tasks are normally expressed as some combination of trial, share, conversion, repeat purchase or weight of purchase related to a target group. For example:

Achieve 20 per cent trial among the 18–25 year old group with a 1.5 litre weight of purchase leading to a 8 per cent market share.

Convert 30 per cent of our current account holders in the $30–50,000 income group to a savings account with a minimum of $5,000 balance.

There is nothing wrong with this, and the fact that the actual results can be measured against these quantified targets is good. But they lack a little inspiration, and understanding of the mechanisms by which this can be achieved. An equally specific task and also one that could be measured could be:

Brief A
Our main task is to make our drink the one that every guy under the age of 25 wants to have in his hand when he's chatting up a girl on a Friday night in a bar or club. Having achieved that, in order to get the sales we want – an 8 per cent market share at a 10 per cent premium – we want him occasionally to buy it during the week or to drink it at home for that 'everyday special' moment. We know the opinions of bar staff and opinion leaders, like style journalists and beer aficionados, are very influential so we want to make sure they buy into the product story and credentials of the drink and recommend it.

Or:

Brief B
We know that the majority of our current account holders have their account with us more by default than choice. We were probably the bank that gave them a student loan or were the nearest bank to where they started their first job. By this stage in their lives, they have a steady partner and are thinking of settling down. They will also be thinking about a savings account but will be more attracted by the specialists. We need to convince them that there is an advantage in having all their business under one roof, and that we are the bank that has all the experts in one place marshalled for their benefit by a personal account manager who really knows them. The personal account manager needs therefore to be the 'hero', and we need to

complement him/her with reassurance about the scale of the bank. In summary, if they believe we are big yet personal, comprehensive but with specialist expertise, we will persuade them to put more of their business with us. Our first task is to get a third of them to open savings accounts, and we'll know they really trust us if they build balances of $5,000 or more.

The point is that the tasks need to be quantifiable but also insightful. You need to know who you are targeting, you need to identify the situations they are in, and you need to work out how attitudes link to behaviour.

The team leader will also have the initial budget, but of course this process is going to give us the possibility of uncovering new ways of investing, which may give us the confidence to ask for more or suggest we need less. Nevertheless, starting with a top-down indication of budget is a prerequisite to providing a bottom up response. As was stressed in the previous section, the revised brief to go into Stage 2 must be for a minimum of a two year plan.

Stage 2: Immersion

This stage is going to end in a workshop for the team from which they will deliver a first cut at a plan. There are five sets of stimuli that will enable them to do this:

- **Brand data** – all the analysis you can get on the brand and its history that relates to the task(s) and that can be unearthed now that the team has defined the tasks so clearly.
- **Consumer touch-points** – you should already have this from the insight stage of the Five 'I's process, but what is required is a clear summary of every way in which your brand interacts with people's lives. Where do they buy it and when do they use it? Where else do they encounter it? Who has opinions about it? How do they store it in the house and how do they dispose of it when they've finished with it? You should explore every single point at which your brand touches people's lives. That's how cereal makers realised that the back of a cornflakes packet should not be wasted on listing the ingredients, but could serve instead as a valuable media space which people read as they munch their breakfast in the morning. Above all, you should find the moments when people's minds are open to messages and persuasion. If you miss an airplane, your mind is open to the use of mobile phones and choice of provider; if you have just had a baby your mind is open to reappraise all sorts of things from insurance to water.
- **Case studies** – somebody somewhere has tried to do what you are trying to do – although maybe not in the same category or country. Find out what

Added Value

they did and try to take some lessons from it. Just two or three good case studies can be really helpful.

- **People passion points** – these are the interests and passions of your target group. They are related to the touch-points but are not necessarily the same, and will be used again when we come to think about an episodic plan.
- **Options** – the team need to be provided with a list and possibly a little information about every possible option at their disposal. Figure 4.6 is a good start and will make the point that the list is longer than one might think.

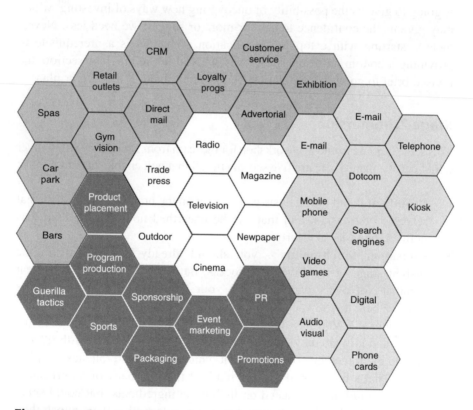

Figure 4.6 Communication channels

Using all this material in a workshop allows for the analytical and the creative: new ideas and new connections achieved by a team of people with different backgrounds and expertise working together. Unfortunately, this rarely seems to happen in 'media planning'.

There is one crucial aspect of this workshop that guarantees it moves a long way from the 60/40 model and every possible option is given a fair hearing. That is the fact every option is reviewed, and is ruled out, not ruled in. In other words, rather than starting with TV ads and seeing what else we might want to do, every option is discussed and a decision is made whether it should be rejected.

We now have a first cut of a plan, which can be captured in a matrix (Figure 4.7).

Task	Target	Activity	Priority	Cost estimate
Awareness among leading edge potential buyers	Opinion-leading men 21–25 years old	Style press Sponsor awards for top young creatives (music, literature, art)	1	$1 million
Recommendation by 'experts'	Bar staff Journalists	Ambassador Programme with bar staff PR editorial Viral Internet campaign	2	$0.5 million
Build respect and admiration	Main target (male)	On premises events in top bars TV and cinema	1	$2.5 million
Position as beer for 'The Mating Game'	Main target (male & female)	SMS text messages of 'best chat-up lines' Cross-promotion with upmarket male fashion retailer	2	$0.5 million
Encourage in-house trial for everyday special	Main target (male)	Special retail pack with 'Party kit' Sponsor special TV movies/ premieres	3	$0.5 million

Figure 4.7 A first plan for a brief

Stages 3 and 4: Expert analysis and Finalising the plan

Most communications planning goes straight from setting the brief and budget to bringing in the experts. But in our plan the previous 'immersion' stage has been inserted into the plan before the experts make their appearance. This is to ensure that the brief the experts work to is rather more comprehensive and imaginative than the ones they normally see.

In the specific area of paid-for media, all the top agencies have quite detailed, mostly computer-based models to determine optimal mixes of expenditure over time (two years, remember). However, the likelihood (or certainty) of this process is that we are going to be required to compare apples with pears – TV and press with events and pack design – so we cannot rely too much on computer modelling. So even with the benefit of some expert analysis, the team is going to have to make some judgement calls to form the final plan.

More than this, in the second and final workshop, the team have to look for the overlaps between the various activities, the linkages and the multiplier effect mentioned earlier:

$$I = f(n \times m \times p)t$$

(the number of times you hear the same message or aspects of it from different people in different places over time increases impact).

Stage 5: Action

The final stage is to write the briefs for the creative teams who have to design the content and the channel and media teams who have to buy. The brief should include the key performance indicators, the deliverables specific to each activity, as well as the media and channels to be used. This will allow performance to be reviewed, adjustments made and lessons learnt for next time.

Of course, working through this process in the exact way described takes the kind of time and commitment that is not often available for developing a 'media and communication plan'. But it should be. After all, we are often talking about millions of dollars of investment here. There is certainly no other expenditure of this magnitude in a business that is subject to so little detailed planning and scrutiny. Poor old factory managers have to do a capital proposal and full business case if they want to spend as little as $50k on a new piece of kit. Sadly, in the world of marketing, millions of dollars of shareholder money can be spent on little more than a whim. Think of the amount of money poured away on sponsorship deals, just because the marketing director has vaguely understood the idea of fame and likes Formula One, or because the chairman is an avid cricket fan.

3. EPISODIC MARKETING

Episodic marketing is a twist on the 360 degree impact plan. It is all about creating that rare and precious thing, word of mouth. The approach was developed by Fusion 5, the American marketing agency that Added Value partnered in 2000. It was successfully used for the launch of Ford's Focus car, which succeeded in making it the number one car for younger drivers and reconnecting Ford to an audience they were in danger of losing. When Jim Schroer, the marketing VP of Ford, moved to Chrysler, he took Fusion with him, and episodic marketing is now being used across the Chrysler range.

The principles of episodic marketing work for any category, but they worked especially well for cars, which had historically adopted the 'launch and abandon' model. Cars take years to develop, and this process is normally controlled by designers and engineers, not by marketers per se. The marketers' job is to launch the car, which they traditionally do with a BIG BANG. There's a dealer conference in an exotic location, a flag-waving ad with the car being driven along some clifftop road to the sound of sexy music, a bit of studious courting of motoring journalists, which will be followed by some press ads and promotions based on free options or no service costs for the first two years. The idea is that every possible buyer hears about the car, sees it in a good light, reads a good review and is finally persuaded to buy because of a great deal. Ad agencies love this because the budgets are huge and they get to work with some very hot directors on the shoot.

Fusion 5 likened this approach to the film *Titanic* – spend a gazillion dollars making it, launch with a blaze of publicity and hope like hell everyone comes to see it. But of course, most of them will come to see it only once. Now, compare the *Titanic* approach to the way *The X Files* works. The series has a basic and very compelling central idea – government conspiracy and aliens. Every episode then focuses on a story that flows from the central idea. It might involve, for example, metamorphosis or mind control. The audience watches every week, and becomes more and more involved with the characters of Mulder and Scully as it does so.

Episodic marketing operates in the same way as *The X Files*. The central idea, in marketing terms, is that the 'brand positioning' and the episodes of the series can be visualised as a series of activity spikes. These spikes are built on ideas that connect the brand positioning to the passion points of the target audience – and they tell a story that involves and engages people. In each spike, all the activity across all the channels, media and promotions is inspired and linked to the main idea for that spike.

Fusion 5 used this technique to great effect in the American campaign for the Ford Focus. In Europe, the Ford Focus is an average family car, but in the United States, Ford wanted to capture the cynical Generation X/Y who had definite preconceptions of Ford cars as boring, bland station wagons, driven by their parents. Ford knew it had to get these young 20-somethings to buy into Ford now, or in ten years' time it wouldn't be selling them any family cars either.

So it got together its key agencies, and under the guidance of Fusion 5, developed an episodic communications plan that aimed to create a real buzz around the new car amongst the core target market. The credo on all proposed activity was, 'If it isn't worth a 20 year old talking about it – don't do it.'

Fusion 5 started by talking to 25 Generation Xers in each of the top five cities, not just to find out their views on Ford and the car market, but to really understand the rest of their lives – what turns them on. They call this DNA immersion – a more holistic view of people which provides the foundation for a plan that actually cuts through and touches them. This delivered a series of passion points – things they were really passionate about – which provided gateways for marketing activities that could connect with this group.

Passion points

Music – live gigs, MTV
Fashion – designer chic that's accessible and youth-focused
Creativity – being a 'creative' making films, TV, ads
Entertainment – *Dawson's Creek* was this target's biggest show
Sport – mountain biking and outdoor pursuits were 'hot'
Technology – audio technology was top of their agenda: in car, in home, portable
Celebrity – accessible, local 'celebs I could meet'.

The next step was to develop an umbrella creative idea that connected the brand to these passion points. This was 'Life is live, so is Focus', a theme which tapped into the 24/7 connected vibe of young people in 2000. From this, Fusion 5 created a series of stirring ideas, each driven out of a particular passion point. Fashion in Focus was one 'spike' which took the well-established link between cars and fashion, but gave it an unexpected and compelling twist. The obvious and uninspiring way to connect to fashion would have been simply to sponsor a show: logos all around, models sitting on bonnets and so on. But Fusion 5 knew this was not going to get young people talking. So it hooked up with *Belle* magazine and asked ten young designers to create outfits out of the materials they found in a Focus – seat belts, seat covers, wires, lamps and so on. The result was an original and provocative fashion show, with Ford as a central player with a real role.

Fusion 5 also realised that Sony was a very aspirational and cool brand for the target group. As Ford already had a radio parts relationship with Sony, it decided to build on this by producing a limited edition vehicle with a kick-ass 450w system – the XPLOD. This in itself was news that made it onto the covers of audio and car magazines – a production car with a sound system usually only fanatics would custom build. But it also tackled the number one problem of how to get 20-year-olds to go down to a Ford dealership. Now with a Focus Sony XPLOD in the showroom, the dealers had queues of them each with a favourite CD in hand, wanting to test drive the sound system. A real result for dealers.

The plan, of course, also contained TV ads, but these were not just any ads, they were the first live adverts shown on network TV for over 20 years. And what's more, they ran a competition on-line for wannabe creatives to write them.

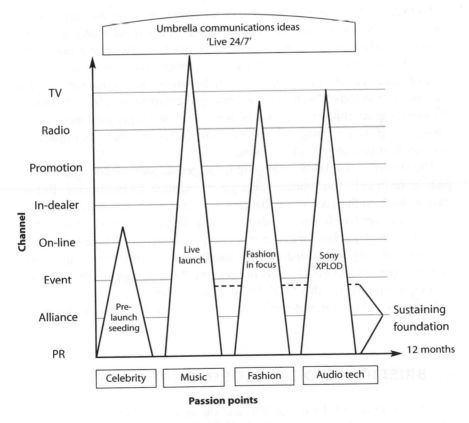

Figure 4.8 Ford Focus episodic plan

One Californian 19-year-old penned a few lines on www.focus247.com and 30 minutes later it was being performed live on national TV. Again Fusion 5 had taken something standard and conventional and made it worth talking about.

In total, the plan spanned 12 months with seven spikes of activity, using a vast array of different media.

A crucial first part of the plan was a pre-launch grass roots 'viral' spike that saw Ford Focuses being given out to trendsetters – DJs, local celebrities and so on – who were seen around town in the top five cities driving something new and different. This created anticipation and buzz among a crucial set of influencers prior to the 'official' launch.

The result of the campaign was that the Ford Focus became the number one car for under 25s in the United States – achieving the seemingly impossible task of making Ford 'cool' again. And as for return on the marketing invest-ment (ROMI), Ford believe it achieved 25 per cent greater impact for 25 per cent less than a conventional communications plan – numbers worth talking about in any business.

So instead of focusing on advertising messages, episodic marketing delib-erately concentrates on activities and events. It is about communicating with people, not advertising at them. Its impact comes from the buzz generated by people talking about a brand with real engagement and enthusiasm. It's the kind of thing that Nigel Bogle meant when he wrote, 'Your competition is life not just other brands.'[6] Well, if we are going to compete with life – what is in the news, big sporting events, rock gods and soap stars, personal traumas and triumphs – if we are going to break through all this and make an impact, we need to do stuff that gets talked about.

The structure of episodic marketing helps people join the dots and find the path to the brand's fundamental message, its big idea, its positioning. But we have to work on the assumption that people are not really that interested in our brand (however wonderful our ads might be). There is so much media activ-ity and so many pitches for our money that people have developed filters and insulation to keep advertising at arm's length. But episodic marketing as part of 360 degree impact offers a way of breaking through people's defences and creating the multiplier effect and the buzz that we seek.

However, to succeed, it demands creative ideas of the highest order within the plan.

4. BRIEFING AND DEVELOPING CREATIVES

The impact plan ended with 'action' and the instruction to 'write the brief'. Well, there is a little more to briefing and ensuring you get great creative work for whatever channels, media and activity is included in the plan. There is in fact several books' worth of best practice here. There is also an industry, the advertising industry, that often behaves as if it wants to keep this as a black art, although it does at least emphasise and encourage good briefs because it is in its interests to do so.

In the spirit of the Five 'I's, let's pick out five things that will make great creative work less of a lottery.

Work with the best

Choose the best agencies and demand the best team in that agency. This is not always easy, but here is one tip for choosing an ad agency that works better than looking at its ad reel. Ask to see every piece of work it has produced for a couple of clients over the period of a year. Then ask to see every piece of work it did for every client in a month. This will show you the breadth and depth of its work. Then arrange to spend a couple of days working on a brief with the team, a hypothetical brief or the real one. This will tell you whether you can work with them and whether the chemistry is right. Ask to see their processes and testimonials from clients who actually use them. This will tell you whether they get good results by luck or luck plus some kind of a system. If you follow this, you will find good agencies, who you can work with and who have a way of replicating success.

Provide a written brief

The brief should be no more than two pages and should cover the following:

- Why do we want new advertising? (The arrival of a new team is not sufficient as an answer!)
- What consumer insight drives this brief?
- Who is our target audience? (This is worth defining extremely clearly.)
- What do they think and do now in relation to our brand and its product category?
- What would we like them to think and do in response to the advertising? (That is, what are the advertising objectives? And how would we measure them – a subject that is much better debated before the advertising runs, than after it.)
- What message is most likely to achieve this change?
- Why should they believe it?
- List any practical considerations for execution.

- Also list the names of the team members, clearly distinguishing the decision maker, who should sign the brief personally.
- Finally, the Brand Bullseye should be attached as an appendix.

It should also have a summary that you could write on a Post-it note. This will force you to give the agency a really clear steer on the deliverable and how you will appraise its work. Bear in mind that the brief has to include some more insight alchemy. Great creative work needs to be fresh, and this requires a fresh insight that might be more precise than the one used to develop the overall brand strategy.

Make the briefing motivating

Your objective, irrespective of your budget or where you sit in the client priorities, is to dominate the thinking time of the creatives, most of which goes on outside normal working hours. Their motivation and passion for the brief is what will make the difference, so don't just e-mail the brief. Speedo did one briefing session in a swimming pool. The marketing director of Guinness in Ireland took the whole agency team on a tour of Ireland for a weekend, involving much drinking of Guinness but also a real immersion in Ireland, young Irish people and the background for the brief.

Define a process and make a plan for how to respond, judge and refine the creative work

The worst moment is when the agency comes back with the 'ideas'. There is often an awkward silence, and then either the most junior or most senior person (the agency doesn't know in advance which) gives a top-of-the-head response based on whether he or she likes it or not. This is not altogether wrong – your first gut reaction will be close to the target audience's, if you have any empathy with them – but there is a better process than this. For example, you can initially respond by asking questions to check you have understood. You can also prepare the agency in advance for the way you will consider the ideas. If you want to go into a huddle or mull it overnight, tell them. You should also be certain that the ideas are being judged against the written brief and not against a brief that is hidden away in the heads of you and your team. As always it is more important that there is a clear process than what that process is. The golden rule – the one that must never be broken – is that he or she who briefs, decides. If the chairman makes the final decision then the chairman must take responsibility for the briefing. Most great creative work is lost because some 'senior person' comes in at the last stage, applies his or her own criteria based on prejudice rather than insight, and cuts across what the team was trying to achieve. It is a great idea to involve senior people – hopefully they are senior because they have experience and good judgement – but then they must lead the process throughout. They should be like the pig and not the chicken in your bacon and eggs – committed and not just involved.

Let the 'consumers' inform your thinking, but don't let them take your decisions

As has been said many times before, consumer research is the big killer of great creative work. However, where possible, ideas should still be explored with people, and this can and should involve quantitative testing. In this testing you are looking for the following:

- Will it make an impact? Will it penetrate, involve and engage?
- Is it fresh? All great creative communications break some kind of rule and present something with a new twist. Häagen Dazs gave away free ice cream at an opera concert in Hyde Park. Apple ran just one ad in the Super Bowl that was unlike any ad for any computer before. There are many examples of this almost indefinable, you-know-it-when-you-see-it, freshness of an idea and/or presentation of an idea.
- Does the message link to the brand?
- Does the message come through?
- Is it convincing? Will it make someone do something different and not just think something different as a result?

When it comes to developing the creative idea, the thing to keep foremost in your mind is that 50 per cent of the power of an idea is in the execution. This applies to anything, but especially to ads. So many of the great ads that we admire are in fact great only as a result of the work done in pre-production. This point is emphasised only because a lot of marketing teams almost switch off after the script is approved. The angel is in the detail. Truly great communication takes a leap at every stage – from the brand idea to the brief, from the brief to the response, from the agreed idea to the execution, but it is very often this last leap that makes the biggest difference. Even in the execution of an event or promotional idea, there is huge top spin to be gained – or pitfalls to be avoided – in the execution. To woo the opera buffs in Hyde Park, the Häagen Dazs team ensured their ice cream was in perfect condition, and also that it was served beautifully by just the right kind of hospitality people.

Finally, be sure that the creative team fully understands the importance of the identity of your brand. All brands need to have consistent design values, and these need to communicate the right things at the right level across the totality of the brand. This means that people should recognise the brand's identity at every point they come into contact with it – so a car manufacturer, for example, should ensure consistency in everything from the look of its showrooms through its advertising and promotional literature to the presentation of its user manual.

This is something that also needs to be considered in terms of a brand's heritage. A glance at the design history of any successful brand will show how it evolves gradually in a way that remains true to the brand's core identity – with some consistent threads such as name, colourways and iconography running through from its launch to the present day. The label on a bottle of Budweiser is instantly recognisable from its key visual signatures – the 'bow tie', the red, white and blue colours – as well as the message that it communicates – its claim to be the 'King of Beers'. But when you look back over the label's 100-year history, it's interesting to notice how this design has evolved incrementally, and also how clearly the ghost of the original label is still present in its very latest incarnation. You'll see the same thing if you park an original 1973 Porsche 911 next to its most recent descendant; they are clearly, in some senses, the same distinctive car, although one looks somehow 'out of date' while the other has clearly benefited from the very latest design and technology.

So, when briefing the creative team, it's crucial that you make it clear which design elements can change (and for what reasons) and which ones need to stay the same. Added Value use a technique called PANDA (Packaging and Design Audit) as an aid to analyse and safeguard a brand's identity. This helps to prepare for writing the creative brief by deconstructing the impact of the brand's design and packaging. First, people are given pencils and paper and are asked to draw the brand. Interestingly, they will almost never get the label or the logo absolutely right, however familiar they are with it. This is important, because you can learn a lot from what they remember about the brand's design and the mistakes that they make in attempting to draw it. When you've done this, start to play around with other design images, labels and logos in the field and see what reactions you get. How recognisable is your brand's name when written in the typeface used by your biggest rival? What values and messages does it communicate now? These kinds of exercise should enable you to identify which aspects of a brand's design are reinforcing its identity and which are distracting from it. The resulting creative brief should then be able to specify the changes that can be made, and the evolution that needs to occur to keep the brand relevant while preserving its core identity.

There is a lot more that could be said on briefing creatives, but just adhering to these simple principles and advice will increase the chance of high impact. And the enticing thought is that most of these measures cost as much to do right as they do to do badly, so it makes sound economic sense to do them well.

5. INTERNAL COMMUNICATIONS

Creating growth which, lest we forget, is the whole point of the Five 'I's process, starts inside the business. The really good brand managers have always understood this. They are not just good at getting an insight on the world, developing an idea, creating innovations, making a plan and briefing creatives – they are fantastic, natural, internal advocates. Their infectious enthusiasm for their brands and their projects gets communicated internally. Only when the enthusiasm for their careers gets in the way (a notorious infection of the infectious) is the impact dulled somewhat.

Every step of the Five 'I's process needs to be thought through from an internal perspective. Who needs to be involved, engaged, and enthused; when and how? When it comes to the brand generally, and a new launch specifically, we need to create impact in the whole business. This is obvious for service businesses like retail, leisure and financial services, because for the most part the people are the brand; but it is true of any business. In the best case studies there is a fantastic moment when you sense the whole company has got it and has got behind it. They know what needs to be achieved and understand their particular role and responsibility.

Alan McWalter, the former marketing director of Marks and Spencer, shows a great video about NASA's Apollo project that brilliantly illustrates the point. We probably all remember the old story of John F Kennedy asking the guy sweeping the floor at NASA what he is doing and being told, 'I'm helping to put a man on the moon.' But Alan's example demonstrates how NASA's teamwork went some way beyond this, by showing the enormous complexity and interdependence of all the experts and technicians. There is a fantastic moment when the rocket is on the launch pad and the people responsible for the every aspect of the mission are asked, in sequence, if they are ready. 'Go – Go – Go – Go – Go!' they all reply, one after the other. As Alan points out, it's a moment when everything has to be absolutely right. There is no way that anyone in the team can say, 'Hang on a second, almost there, just give me a moment!' Any problems with NASA's internal communications would have meant, quite literally, disaster.

Internal impact is not needed only for the brand-related activity. Every business has big messages it needs to get across all the time – a new IT system, a change of ownership or any new strategic focus for example, all of which potentially bring new opportunities if only we can overcome internal cynicism, apathy, inertia, conservatism, clutter and get the message across.

There has been great progress in internal communications in recent years. Many businesses now have a functional expert, and there are specialist agencies they can work with that fulfil the role ad agencies traditionally supplied for external communications. But, sadly, the majority of internal communications is still low grade, ineffective and gets nowhere near the impact of a mission to the moon. There is an incredible lack of imagination in most internal communications, particularly when you compare them with external communications. Step outside the workplace and you become a 'consumer', treated to all manner of wonderful and ingenious methods of communication. Step back in the workplace and you get the company conference and the house magazine.

I remember once working with a large risk management firm. We had completed a series of internal workshops and stakeholder interviews, and were feeding back the less than good news of how well the company's strategic message had been understood. You could see the boss getting more and more frustrated as he heard the findings until finally, unable to contain himself, he interrupted the meeting and produced the latest copy of the company magazine. 'I just don't understand why they don't get it. Read what I said in this lead article, it could not have been clearer.' Well it could, actually.

There is one overwhelming reason why most internal communications are poor: companies do not put the same investment and discipline into internal communications as they do into external. Apart from being prepared to put in the time and money and give it the priority, there are five specific things that can put this right.

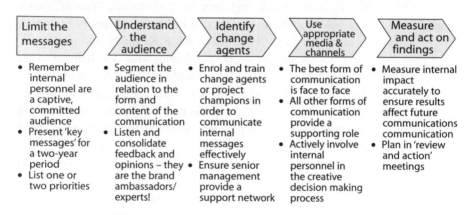

Figure 4.9 Five ways to put internal communications right

Limit the messages

There is an old trick for teaching young marketers the discipline of writing creative briefs for an external audience. You get one of them up front, throw five tennis balls at them, and watch them drop some, if not all of them. Then you throw the marketer just one tennis ball, and of course he/she catches it. This is a neat way of making the point that external communications should have just one main message. But the situation is slightly different with an internal audience. Since they are both captive and committed – at least to some degree – they probably can just about catch five tennis balls. After all, most people come to work wanting to do a good job, and are receptive to any messages that point them in the right direction. But even with an internal audience, remember that five messages is pretty much the maximum.

There were some nice ironies for the team that developed Unilever's Advanced Brand Communications initiative which, for the most part, was a best practice case study in internal communications. For one thing, the initiative itself contained many more than the few clear messages ABC calls for when writing a brief for external communications. It was also not branded very well, and the team were not able to take much account of what else Unilever was trying to communicate internally at the time. Internal communications has to operate within an overall plan that looks at all the 'key messages' for a two-year period. Five is a good number of messages, but within this there needs to be some sense of priority, to make it clear which one or two are the most important.

Understand and segment the audience

You may feel you know your internal people well, but you have to understand them in the context of what you are trying to communicate. You also have to be able to segment them, to know precisely what message needs to be given to which group in which way. There is one golden rule to follow here that marks a difference from external research. In internal research, the research is communication. The very fact that you are asking people opinions, the way you ask them and the feedback they get from the output of the research matter, because it is their company, their brand. Of course in theory, you could make the same argument for 'consumers', but the truth is that there are many millions more of them out there, so you can afford to put a few in the goldfish bowl and then toss them back in the ocean. After all, in the final analysis they are not quite as fixated on your brand as you are.

Identify and use change agents

Just as in external communications, we should always look for the opinion leaders and single them out for special treatment, because they can get the message across better than any didactic ad. In internal communications, the best approach is to enrol and train them to be the bearers of the message. Even in a company of many thousands of employees, leading the internal communications with just 30 carefully selected 'ambassadors' or 'champions' or 'change agents' is the best approach. What follows should be led by them and supported by senior management.

Use the appropriate media and channels, and use them in combination

The best communication is face to face, just like the best advertising is word of mouth, but it is much easier to achieve this internally. All the other forms of communication have a role in supporting this – the conference, the cascade briefings, the magazines, the posters in the canteen – but face to face, two way communication is the most involving. This kind of thinking can be applied even to large internal audiences. With one client we took 200 of its senior managers to an empty warehouse in London's Docklands. They received a keynote address to set the context and were given lots of raw materials – big screens, paint, video cameras, all manner of props – and asked to create the vision for the business and how it related to all the key activities, processes and functions. The energy was amazing and the output better than anything that could have been dreamt up by your favourite conference organiser, simply because they were all involved.

Measure findings and act on them

Most companies do not measure internal impact, or if they do it is in the most perfunctory way, and it is not obvious how the results affect future communications. You need to know, have you changed attitudes and behaviours?

Personally I am a sucker for the big and even the silly signifiers of change: the 'gimmicks' that ram it home that the business is serious. Big displays in the foyer, little executive toys that sit on your desk reminding you of the key messages in the mission statement. I recently saw a great one in action – it was a series of mats positioned around the office, which related to the changes in behaviour everyone had been told were crucial to achieve growth. For example one mat said, 'Stand on this if you have taken a risk today.' An electronic counter recorded the number of risk takers. It certainly makes an impact – although only in the context of a planned and sustained programme of internal communications.

If there is just one tennis ball to catch it really is to ensure that the Five 'I's process – insight, idea, innovation, impact and investment return – is applied internally to affect the behaviours necessary to create growth.

I was once asked to run a strategy workshop for the board of a medium-sized spirits business (the kind you drink, not the kind you exorcise). We discussed

the 'habits of successful growth businesses' and they completed a spider graph
like the one in Figure 4.10 to assess themselves.

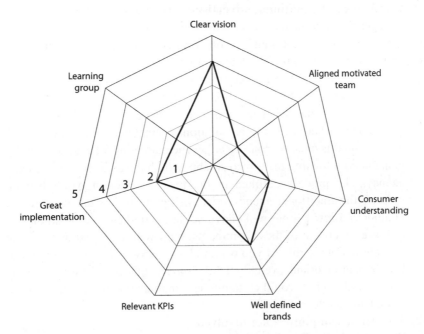

Figure 4.10 A spider graph for the habits of successful growth businesses

As you can see, the board were very self-critical, awarding themselves low
scores in virtually every category. At the end of the discussion, one of the
directors asked me, 'We can't do everything at once, so which one or two
things would you tackle first?'

My immediate answer was that they should address the values and vision
of the company. After all, I reasoned, if you point people in the right direction,
they should be able to start figuring out which steps to take for themselves.
But it occurred to me on the plane home that this was only half the answer to
their question. Changing the vision and values of a company will only work if
you change the metrics as well. If you change the direction of a company, it is
imperative that you change the measures by which you judge progress towards
your new destination. If a rugby team sets itself the challenge of becoming
impregnable in defence, it will measure its success by the number of tackles it
makes; if a soccer team is focused on all-out attack, it will measure the number
of attempts on goal. So how does a business align its vision and its metrics?

That is a question that brings us to the fifth and final 'I' of marketing
alchemy: investment return.

THE STUFF THAT GETS IN THE WAY OF IMPACT

1. Dominance of traditional advertising and media agencies

Ad agencies and media agencies do a great job – in the area of paid-for advertising. One creates and the other buys. However, the simple fact is that impact needs to be 360 degree, involving things other than paid-for advertising, and ad/media agencies are lousy coordinators of this. It does not matter whether this is because of vested interest or lack of skill sets, it matters that it is true, and if it is changing, it is changing at a snail's pace. There needs to be solution/channel/budget neutral coordination, and this must be done by either the marketing VP and/or an independent coordinating team who sit above both the ad agency and media agency. The process outlined in the previous section won't happen through the traditional agency relationships to the extent it needs to. Doubtless a few people will shove some contradictory case studies in my face as a result of these comments, but I will reply that they are the exception, not the rule. If you want to know why 'half is wasted' and so few brands or brand events get full impact, this is the biggest single cause – although it would certainly help matters if their clients learnt to write halfway decent briefs.

2. The whole company is not involved

Occasionally you see a whole business get behind a launch, with everyone including the factory and finance people out in the stores distributing samples or just doing whatever it takes. It cannot be the case that this new army of in-store merchandisers really makes a material difference to the trial rates, but it is the case that something magical happens to the whole process of creating impact when every single person in the business finds some role in its creation. I have never seen it fail, and I think this is because somehow it removes the option of failure – there is just too much riding on it.

3. No big flags

Adam Morgan of eatbigfish., an agency that specialises in helping challenger brands puts it well:

> *Successful challenger brands are brands in a hurry; they desire (and need to) puncture the consumer's autopilot and create reappraisal ... to do so, they create big impactful acts or marketing ideas that capture the indifferent consumer's imagination and bring about a rapid re-evaluation of their image in the consumer's mind and role in the consumer's life.*[7]

Apart from the use of the word 'consumer' (they're people, that's why they have lives that make them indifferent to some brands) and the implication (probably unintended) that this applies only to challenger brands and only externally, Adam has it spot on. If you want to change and make it obvious you have changed, you have to create some obvious flag of change and run it up the flagpole both inside the company and outside on the highest rooftop you can find. He gives an example from the US motor industry:

> *The radical designs of the Dodge Viper and Plymouth Prowler were not intended to sell a lot of cars, they were intended as a signal to the world (and themselves) that here was a company that was about to become very different.*

4. No multiplier
Impact needs the multiplier – the effect of lots of different events and messages (within the same theme) happening together and over time – to create the 'tipping point'. This needs to be managed and created. It can happen by luck but it can be manufactured. Most 'marketing campaigns' are anything but.

5. No learning, no pain – no pain, no gain
Most businesses simply fail to learn between one launch and the next. We only ever did one project which sought to identify how different aspects of the marketing activity worked, and how they worked together. It was a modest project to investigate store opening campaigns for a grocery retail chain. The company surrounded the openings with the usual marketing effort – local PR, press ads, staff briefings and so on. But it turned out the biggest impact was created by the blimp that flew above the new store for the week before and weeks after opening.

Of course, the impact of the blimp has to be taken in the context of how all the other elements, including the involvement of the staff, worked together. The blimp was merely a symbol of the multiplier effect in action: proper coordination, the whole company involved and an appetite to learn, all in one example.

CHAPTER 5

Investment Return

The investment return in sport is clear. It comes in the form of championships, cups and trophies, as well as sponsorship deals and prize money. The powerful motivation to win means that professional sports teams, sports stars and their back-up staff are some of the most ruthless and effective learning organisations around. In comparison, many businesses look like the committee of the local church bazaar.

So how did sport turn from a jolly game into a clash of winning machines? Measurement is perhaps one of the key factors. Degrees of success in sport can be calibrated exactly, and the reasons for that success can be measured precisely too. It can be broken down into goals, tries and points on the board – which can be broken down further still into tackles made, possession retained, approaches to the net or passing shots. Both in business and in sport, the measurement and analysis of success are crucial for one simple reason: what gets measured, gets done.

Measurement is about more than just keeping score. It is one of the foundations of success which, in business terms of course, means profitable top-line growth. Too often, investment return is thought of as the end point – the goal of growth. But just because it's the last 'I' in the book does not mean it's the last in the process. Remember, the Five 'I's is not a linear progression, it's a loop that you can supercharge from anywhere. In fact, in many cases investment return will be the starting point, since it can be a rich source of insights.

But the marketer should be passionate about investment return for another reason, too. To put it bluntly, growth will only happen when marketers learn how to make the case for investing in ways the finance director and the CEO can understand. Does that sound like too much to ask?

It's tough for a marketer. You have to be intuitive and analytical, logical and imaginative, a great strategist, a great implementer and a great communicator. You have to be able to inspire sales teams, researchers, designers and creatives. You need to be a great staff manager, a leader and a team member. You're the one with the big picture but you're also the details person. You're as much an expert on the science as you are on the 'consumer'. You're a guardian and an innovator, and yes, you're also someone who can make an investment case. But this is why marketing is the best job in the world – you are the quarterback, the rugby fly half, the David Beckham, the Ian Botham, the Magic Johnson – you get to make it happen.

These days, you don't often hear a brand manager referred to as the 'managing director of the brand'. This is a great shame, because it was the basis of the brand management system invented by Procter & Gamble, and it was what used to attract so many of us to become brand managers. The idea of effectively running your own small business, of being at the centre of everything connected with the brand, and of having huge influence over all other functions in the business, is what appealed to the ambitious graduate in the 1960s and 1970s. As a brand manager in a top marketing business like Procter, Unilever, Mars or Nestlé, you believed you were on the path to the very top. When I joined Levers, the joke was that the best way to get rid of a brand manager was to whisper in his ear that he would never make chairman. In fact, it was not far short of the truth. I can recall several who did indeed leave because it was made clear that in ten years' time they would not be running one of the operating companies. And those that stayed all did indeed go on to become chairmen of businesses in the empire.

But companies like Procter and Unilever, where being a great marketer is likely to take you to the very top of the business, are now the exception rather than the rule. The majority of chairmen are financial people, and marketing is certainly not a guaranteed route to the board. In fact, most boards of major businesses don't even have marketing directors on them. What went wrong?

The marketing community's explanation is that boards and shareholders do not understand or sufficiently value brands. This is plainly not true. As has been said before, the majority of a business's stock market value lies in its intangible assets, and the majority of this is in the value of its brands. Of course, shareholders know this full well. So what is it then that they don't understand? Is it that they just don't understand marketing? Or perhaps they don't value it as a central business discipline? Or perhaps they can't see that when you strip away access to capital (human and financial) and the supply chain, the guts of corporate strategy is marketing strategy? And if they really don't understand this, whose fault is it?

My view is that the fault lies squarely at the door of marketing and marketers. For too long, we haven't made a proper financial case, and we have failed to link brand-building to shareholder value in the way other investments are linked. Instead this has been sacrificed for the pseudo-science of branding, which is flimsy and jargon-ridden. If you aspire to be the chairman, then like the chairman you have to be able to speak in financial terms.

If you looked at the titles for the Five 'I's process and found investment return the least appetising, then you miss the point. This is the part of the process that unlocks insight, makes it happen and gets access to the money. Get this bit right and you deserve to get paid as much as the investment banker – but, believe me, you'll have a lot more fun.

So in this chapter, we are going to cover six areas:

- Key performance indicators
- Brand health
- Brand vitality
- GAME plans
- Brand valuation.

Just kidding. You're right, it's five.

1. KEY PERFORMANCE INDICATORS

The dashboard of your car might look like the flight deck of the Starship Enterprise, but let's be honest, who really uses all those meters, lights and dials? If you're in a speed check zone, you check the speedometer. If you're stuck in traffic in 45 degree heat, you probably keep an eye on the temperature gauge. But unless you think you're Michael Schumacher, the tachometer, oil pressure indicator and hydraulic fluid level lights probably don't concern you overmuch.

The point is that when you drive a car, you focus on the one indicator that is most appropriate to your current situation, and the same should be true in business. Most businesses measure a lot of things, but there is normally a dominant key performance indicator – or KPI – that links to the strategy and the company's particular view of the market.

Earlier in the book we saw how Guinness Ireland changed strategy and unlocked growth by changing the dominant KPI from share of stout to share of throat, and particularly share of younger throats. We also saw how, for many years, Coke relentlessly pursued dominance of per capita consumption, before moving into a redefined market that has resulted in non-cola innovation. It's easy to be critical, but had Coke moved earlier it might have been the one to create Sunny Delight, Snapple and Red Bull.

At my alma mater, Levers, I had the privilege of working for one of the finest chairmen I have ever met, Len Hardy. Len was a clear strategic thinker, a good communicator and a ruthless implementer. We competed in eight product categories in household cleaning, but three of them were high growth potential. Two of these were driven by the new automatic washing machines that were coming onto the market – everyone in the UK has them now, but in the mid-1970s, penetration was only 20 per cent. These two products were new detergents (so-called low suds powders) and fabric conditioners; the third high growth potential product was liquid abrasives for work surfaces. Ah … it was a romantic category. Len was a disciple of BCG categories, and his three brands, Persil Automatic, Comfort and Jif respectively, were his stars. His strategy was simple – keep the prices and the margins tight and the investment high, dominate the market with 50 per cent shares, and grow with the market. Every single person in the business including, with no exaggeration, his chauffeur knew the plan and the priorities.

I am proud to say I worked on all three brands in succession, and in each there was only one KPI, volume share. Forget value share or profits. Volume share was the only true measure that the strategy was working. In fact, Lever was much more sophisticated than this sounds. We had an excellent team of econometricians and we could model the share to take out the effect of any price discounting, promotions and advertising. This would give us the equilibrium share – the share we would have had, all other things being equal. We were also able to calculate the exact price relationship with competitors that we needed to achieve the highest volume for the highest profit. But when you met Len in the lift, he would always ask you, 'What's your volume share?' He actually knew, he always had the data delivered to him first, but he wanted to know if you knew. The only time I was caught out, I replied, 'Not as high as it's going to be.' And got away with it. Just that once.

The point of the anecdote is that Levers is the only business I have ever come across where the chairman made it his personal business to ensure that the whole company knew the strategy and was fixated by the right KPI. To be honest, it is one of the few that had such a clear strategy. By the way, during the late 1970s and early 1980s Lever UK beat Procter in seven out of the eight household cleaning categories (it never did succeed in beating Fairy dishwash). It was the only business in Unilever with such a dominant position versus Procter, and it was always a reliable and star profit performer.

But in most businesses, even if there is a clear strategy, the CEO could not tell you factually whether a) the strategy was understood and b) the dominant KPI, the one people really worked to achieve, was aligned to that strategy. He really should be able to. If a business claims that its strategic vision is to be the number one in its industry for customer care, then it needs to make sure that everyone in the company focuses on the KPI that measures success in that particular area. It is no good claiming to be the number one in customer care if all your employees are fixated on achieving short term profits.

Auditing the link between strategic vision and KPI is utterly straightforward. It can be done internally but it is probably better to use some objective consultants to do it for you; although it's such an easy thing to do that if they charge you more than $50k, you can be certain they are ripping you off. Remember they are not being asked to comment on whether the strategy or KPI is right, they are just being asked to provide the answers to three questions (not even five!):

- What do people think the strategy is?
- Which KPI do they think the board and the CEO care about?
- Are the strategy and the KPIs aligned?

The process should begin with a vision audit to understand how the company communicates its vision internally and what its staff understand that vision to be. This can be done by reviewing the company's internal communications (company newsletters, memos to staff and so on) and interviewing or conducting focus groups with employees. Next, you need to talk to the senior team in the company and ask them what they believe the vision for the business to be and which KPIs are most effective in measuring it. For example, if the vision for the business is to become more brand-oriented, clearly brand measurement tools should be selected to monitor the main KPIs.

Having agreed a process and a method for collecting data, you should then start to look at how well the staff understand the KPIs. This can be done through interviews, but it's also important to check the quality of your information by shadowing staff during their working day. You may be told that the dominant KPI is a customer satisfaction rating, but discover that this is rarely mentioned at staff meetings – a sure sign of misalignment. Also, look at the management information systems to see how these deal with the main

KPIs. Management will often measure everything that moves in a business, but it is important that they focus on the data that really matters. You'll also need to do some quantitative research at this point to provide some figures to show what people think the vision of the business is and what the KPIs are. This can be done very simply, by letting people choose from a series of vision statement alternatives, or by getting them to rank KPIs in order of importance.

The results of all this research can then be fed back to the senior team. They may perhaps find that there is a considerable gap between what the vision is intended to be and how people understand that vision. Or they could find that the interpretation of the vision and the KPIs is inconsistent across the company. Whatever the conclusions, this research can then be fed into a GAME plan (of which more later), and progress to rectify any inconsistencies or misalignments can then be tracked through an ongoing internal audit process.

Monitoring your dominant KPI is an excellent way of focusing the business on the right kind of growth, and checking that the growth targets are being achieved. But to measure your brand's performance properly, you'll need some more precise methods of analysis, which means doing a thorough brand health check.

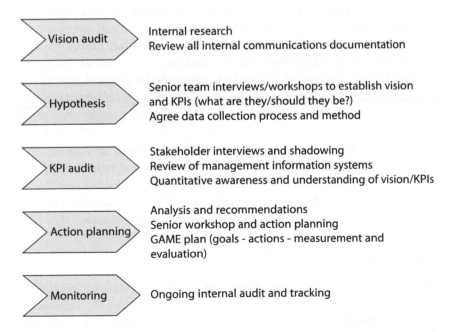

Figure 5.2 Vision and KPI audit

2. BRAND HEALTH

If you go to the doctor for a check-up, the first thing he will do is weigh and measure you, then take your pulse and your blood pressure. From these simple measures the doctor can tell a lot about your basic health. In marketing, we look at share and UVG (underlying volume growth), penetration and repeat purchase. And you can tell a lot about a brand from these simple measures. Which is just as well, because that's about all the marketing information that ever seems to penetrate the boardroom.

If you paid your $250 for the Wellperson check-up, you'd feel a little short changed if all the insight you got was 'a little overweight for your height, but your heart is fine'. But that's not all the doctor does. The experienced medical team – I'm talking private sector here – carry out a series of tests that diagnose and then make a prognosis. They use surrogate measures and they have a point of view, based on science, of how the surrogates – the things they can measure easily from a simple blood or urine test – and all the other tests connect. This gives them a reading on your condition, your capabilities and the risks you face if you do not make changes. Armed with this information – how the inputs in terms of diet, exercise and drugs relate to the outputs (your health), you can make decisions.

Sadly, marketing is still locked in the height and weight school of brand health, despite two decades of effort by consultants and researchers. The more advanced ways of assessing brands have never been integrated, and there seems to be no industry-agreed way of showing how the various measures relate to each other. The foundation of investment return is an analysis of how the inputs in terms of marketing investment and management relate to the outputs in terms of health and profit returns, but this crucial aspect of marketing still remains a murky art rather than a clear science.

So, starting with some simple measures, we are going to work through a model for brand health that truly assesses, diagnoses and prognoses. We will avoid the modelling and the econometrics, let's leave that for another day. Instead we will try to keep it simple and clear so that anyone can understand it, and most importantly, so that a finance director can understand it.

The basics

The place to start is with how much you are selling and what revenue and profit you are getting, compared with what you are spending. You also need to know what direction this is moving in, using either compound annual growth (CAGR) or moving annual totals (MAT). More specifically:

Volume, Revenue and Profit CAGR
The ratio between profit and marketing expenditure on a three-year MAT.

(Here the MAT has to be at least three years because we are looking for an under-lying trend, and we don't want to be confused by one, possibly exceptional, year.)

The comparisons

Next we need to find out how this benchmarks, so first, we look at **market share**. Of course, the problem is: which market do you look at? Is it the one in which you are always brand leader – the market for German sports cars beginning with the letter P – or the one that represents some kind of consideration set for people – the import car market, or just the car market? If in doubt, look at them all.

Notwithstanding the story of Lever's fixation with volume share, which was the right KPI for a particular strategy at a moment in time, we should look at **both volume share and value share**. If the volume is lower than the value or vice versa, and if there is a widening or narrowing gap, this starts to tell you something. In theory, a higher volume share than value share means that you are commanding less of a price premium than your competitors. No problem if you are an economy brand, but a big problem if you aspire to be a premium brand.

To confirm this, **look at price index versus competitors**. In Chapter 2, Ideas, when looking at the reason for under-indexing or over-indexing versus a particular segment, we advanced a number of possible reasons for under-performance. Perhaps your products are not available, or they are but people are not aware of them. Or perhaps people are aware but the products are considered to be too expensive, the wrong format, or to have the wrong bene-fits or image. These issues form the basis for a diagnosis that will go some way to explain the basic scores and the comparisons.

The diagnosis

Your customers' experience of your brand can be likened to a journey that starts with awareness and, hopefully, ends up with them falling in love with your brand. Of course, many of them won't actually see the journey through to its end – the 'love' part is the hardest – but your job is to understand why this does or doesn't happen. To do this, first set out the key facts that map your customers' journey.

What percentage of people are aware of your brand?

Unless people are aware of your brand they can't even start the journey, so you're obviously hoping to find a high figure here. And it's also worth looking at the figures for both spontaneous and prompted awareness, as the difference between the two can be very revealing. A much higher prompted than spontaneous score tells you that you are losing it – losing clout, saliency, influence. Remember Donny Osmond? Apparently he is still making records.

How many people have tried the brand or have considered buying it?

As discussed in the chapter on Impact, awareness needs to be converted into action. Everyone in the world may know that you make a fantastic car, but that may still not be enough to get them into the showroom, behind the wheel and out for a test drive.

How many use it sometimes or often?

Hopefully, once people have tried your brand, they'll start to use it regularly. If that's not the case, you need to find out why not.

How many really love it?

Of course, what you really want are people like those hairy Harley-Davidson fans who are prepared to tattoo your logo on their chests, but there are plenty of other ways of showing passion for a brand. Is it an irreplaceable part of people's lives? Do they recommend it to their friends? Will they forgive its mistakes and celebrate its successes?

The figures you get from answering these questions will highlight your brand's strengths and weaknesses. A quick glance at the journey of the hypothetical brand in the chart shows immediately that its strengths are that a high proportion of people who try the brand go on to use it (a conversion ratio of 75 per cent) and a very high proportion of those people really love it (66 per cent). The problem for the brand is that only half the people who are aware of the brand have tried it or are considering it.

When you've considered the facts that map the journey into the brand, you need to understand the opinions that people hold about the brand – in particular, under the following headings:

- **Value.** Are you considered good (poor or excellent) value for money, and how does this compare between people who buy you and people who don't?
- **Respect.** Is your brand credible? Do people believe the claims you make for it? What kind of status does it have?

	Aware	Consider/try	Use occasionally	Use regularly
% of target user group	80%	40%	30%	20%
Conversion ratio		50	75	66
% of sample agreeing that brand is...				
good value	60% of 80%	70% of 40%	65% of 30%	85% of 20%
a brand I respect	40%	40%	50%	75%
relevant to my needs	50%	50%	40%	80%
different	30%	10%	20%	50%
the best at e.g. efficiency	10%	15%	15%	30%
becoming more popular	5%	5%	10%	15%
a brand I would recommend	5%	5%	10%	30%

Figure 5.3 Journey into the brand

- **Relevance.** Do people perceive your brand as being relevant to their needs?
- **Difference.** How distinctive are you? How well differentiated are you from your competitors?
- **Performance.** In what areas is your brand considered to perform well, or to excel? Is it, for example, the most efficient in its market?
- **Popularity.** Do people think that your brand is becoming more or less popular?
- **Recommendation.** Would they recommend it to others?

These opinions are what will drive people through their journey from awareness to adoration. But the tricky part of the process is to understand how and when these opinions translate into meaningful progress from one stage of the journey to the next. The figures in Figure 5.3, for example, show that the brand is generally perceived to be good value and relevant, even among those who have never tried it. As you would expect, the percentages are higher in all cases for those who really love the brand, but even among these people, some big problems show up in the bottom two rows. Why does such a tiny minority believe that the brand is becoming more popular? And why would so few people – even among its devotees – recommend it to others? The job of the marketer here is to identify the opinions that really make a difference to customers' behaviour.

Having done this, you're in a position to mark up a brand scorecard, setting out the inputs and the outputs of your business. On the input side, this will help you to see how much money you're spending on the brand, the mix of how you're spending it, the pricing and availability of your products, and you'll also be able to check that your customers are experiencing your product or service in the way that you intend. On the output side, you should set out your CAGR (compound annual growth rate) for revenue, volume and profit, as well as your value share and volume share. You should also look at the two key ratios for determining your return on marketing investment (ROMI).

When you look at the investment that you're making in a brand, you need to benchmark it not just against other brands in your category, but also against what the top brands in other fields are spending. This will allow you to determine how much attention you command in your own product or service category (share of voice) as well as how much attention you command among the public in general (share of ear). You should also think about the quality of your investment; ask yourself whether the money is producing the content that you really want and whether you're spending it on the right things. For example, if a large percentage of your marketing budget is being absorbed by a sponsorship deal, you may want to question whether that deal is delivering all that it should in terms of the impact that it produces.

Brand inputs

MARKETING SPEND

	Last 3 Years	Current year
As % of category (share of voice)	20%	10%
Index to Top 10 national brands (share of ear)	85	65

PRICING

	Target index	Actual index
To a) Market average	105	100
b) Designated competitor brand	115	110

QUALITY

E.g. Blind preference to key competitor 70/30
E.g. Service delivery indicators

DISTRIBUTION

E.g. % availability 85%

Brand outputs

	MOVING ANNUAL TOTAL BASED ON:				
	3 year average	1 year	Last 6 months	Last 3 months	
Revenue	$150	$170	$170	$165	
Volume/ unit sales	15m	16.5m	16m	15.5m	
Operating profit	$30	$34	$30	$25	
Value share	10%	11%	10%	9%	
Volume share	12%	11%	12%	10%	

	Last 3 Years	Current year
Marketing spend as % of revenue	8%	5%
Marketing spend as % of profit	75%	50%

If a service brand consider:
Average weight of spend
Average services bought
Cost per customer acquired

Figure 5.4 The brand scorecard

Next, look at your pricing policy to see if it's optimal for the markets that you're targeting, by indexing it against both the market average and a designated key competitor. Then, think about the quality of your product or service in terms of the benefits it provides, your customer service or whichever indicator is most appropriate to your category. Finally, assess the effectiveness of your distribution.

Once you've gone through the inputs, look at the outputs. As already mentioned, here you're considering CAGR revenue, volume, profit, plus value and volume share. However, you also need to consider two other key ratios. The ratio of marketing investment to revenue will tell you how much of the public's money your investment is producing, while the ratio of investment to profit growth will indicate how much of that is turned into profit. It is important that both ratios should be looked at together, because it is quite possible to have high profit growth on low revenues, and to have high revenues but low profit growth – both of which would be undesirable outcomes.

At the level of brand health assessment, there is only one further piece of analysis that needs to be done, which is to look at your share of new market entrants. In almost every case, this means the younger person. Is your share of people coming into your market higher or lower than your overall share? If it is lower, alarm bells should ring all around the business, as they do in markets like fashion and drinks. In these markets, they know their future depends on the young.

These measures are the basic building blocks, and you might think this is kindergarten stuff. But just ask yourself, how often does the leadership team sit down, review and take actions on all the measures? If it is just once a year, this does not compare very well with all those successful sporting teams. Nor does it demonstrate great diligence in the stewardship of more than 50 per cent of the company's shareholder value.

Recruitment in service brands

There is a particular way of looking at recruitment in service brands and of making the link to shareholder value. The 'Holy Trinity' in service brands are – low cost of customer acquisition, high propensity for those customers to cross purchase, and a low attrition rate. This recognises the greater ebb and flow of customers and the wide range of competing specialists in a typical service industry. It is an interesting feature of many service industries that you can 'sample the product' for free just by walking in (if it's a shop or a hotel). The prize is to get them to spend, spend lots and stay forever for the least amount of expenditure.

I have noticed that marketing directors in service industries are often anxious for a simple way to explain how their work relates to the work of their non-marketing colleagues. Figure 5.5 sets out the ideal situation.

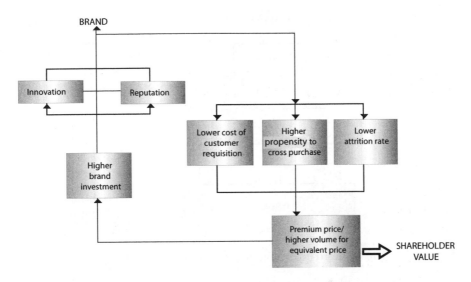

Figure 5.5 The link between brands and shareholder value: service brands

Just as many of the marketing measures that developed in FMCG have relevance to service industries, so this analysis can be adapted to product brands, particularly the ones that have range-extended on the assumption that there is some economy of scale in 'leveraging the brand'. If this is true, you would expect to see the scores improve for customer acquisition, cross purchase and attrition.

BrandDynamics™

There are thousands of more sophisticated ways of measuring brand health on offer from various institutes and consultancies. But nothing in any way approaching an industry standard has yet been established, so you simply pay your money and make your choice. But, for what it's worth, one of my favourites is BrandDynamics™ which was developed by Millward Brown, a business that has a lot of experience in the field. The basic principle is to track the progress of a brand from awareness through to purchase. As the pyramid below shows, the foundation is presence. After all, you can't buy something if you don't know about it, and there is no point being famous if nobody buys you. Then, the brand moves through a number of stages until a person starts to feel a strong bonding or commitment to it. This can sometimes be a nanosecond decision, and sometimes be the result of long and careful consideration.

This model is designed to measure the efficiency with which a brand achieves

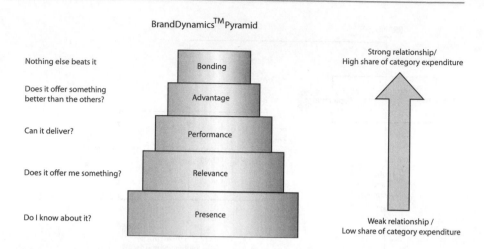

Figure 5.6 The Millward Brown BrandDynamics™ Pyramid

this conversion. Strong brands have the ability to convert awareness to purchase, via all the key stages, more efficiently than weak brands; that is to say, there is less wastage along the way. The ratio of marketing investment to this conversion is a fundamental measure of the return on marketing investment.

BrandDynamics is certainly another useful piece of vocabulary in the marketer's financial lexicon. But are we ready to speak to the finance director yet, in terms he or she would appreciate? Well, I'd say we're starting to get somewhere. But let's not forget it's not just our job to check and prod the patient, we've also got to bring this brand to life.

3. BRAND VITALITY

There is a difference between health and vitality. Healthy people have regular check-ups, take sensible amounts of exercise and go on the cabbage soup diet after Christmas every year. Vital people are the ones who smash their racquets against the squash court wall and make an exhibition of themselves at their salsa class.

We know it's important for a brand to be in good health – and we've just looked at some ways of measuring this. But what we're really looking for in a brand is boundless energy and the potential to run and run. How the hell do you measure that?

Over the years at Added Value, we developed a system for measuring brand vitality. Its governing principle is the need to measure not just current health, but far more importantly, fitness to face the future. The key component is a relatively large-scale quantitative study, where users and non-users of the key brands in a market assess them on a wide range of measures related to brand health. These measures are combined to provide a summary of both the brand's current equity and its future momentum – and it is the combination of equity and momentum that constitutes overall vitality.

The list of factors in the questionnaire was derived initially from our experience of what drives consumers' perception of brands across a wide variety of markets. From this, we worked out a common set of measures so we could compare across markets. The measures are then grouped under those that indicate current equity and those that measure future momentum. In turn, these are broken down into not five, but six (!) 'R's to provide an overall model for brand vitality.

In Figure 5.7, each R reflects a series of questions in the questionnaire, which cover the following broad areas:

- Recognition: being well-known, awareness of the brand's logo and its perceived scale and size.
- Reputation: what the brand stands for in the minds of target consumers
- Relevance: does what the brand offers correspond to what people want?
- Relationship: is it part of people's lives and not just on their shopping list?
- Recruitment: does it attract new users and is it expected to innovate in areas which are important to consumers?
- Rejuvenation: does it retain existing new users and is it likely to do new things which meet their future needs?

The analysis generates not only an overall vitality score, but also an equity and momentum score and then a score for each of the 'R's. The distinction between equity and momentum and between the different 'R's and 'M's which make up these overall measures can be used to diagnose the brands in a particular market, as you can see in Figure 5.8.

Here, Brand A is strong on current equity but has poor momentum, so while awareness and share may be high at the moment, there are warning signs that it may struggle both to retain its current users and to recruit new ones. By contrast, Brand B is a brand that seems to be on a roll, with good equity and momentum. Brand C would typically be a young brand that has not yet established its current equity as well as the others, but is clearly building momentum.

In Figure 5.9 the scores have been broken down further, to focus on equity. It becomes apparent that Brand A is relatively strong on memorability, but less so on motivation. This is quite common among brands that have been around for some time, but are now living on their reputations and not doing enough to build relationships with their customers or to remain relevant to their needs

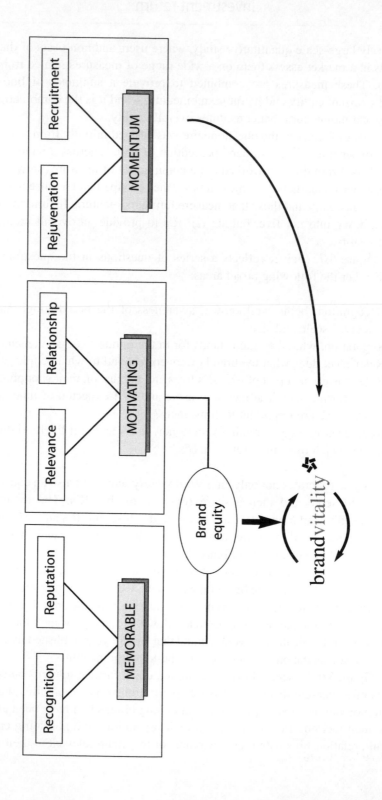

Figure 5.7 Brand vitality 1

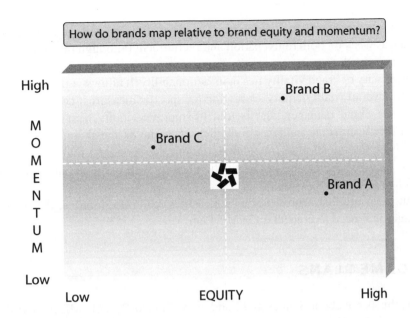

Figure 5.8 Brand vitality 2

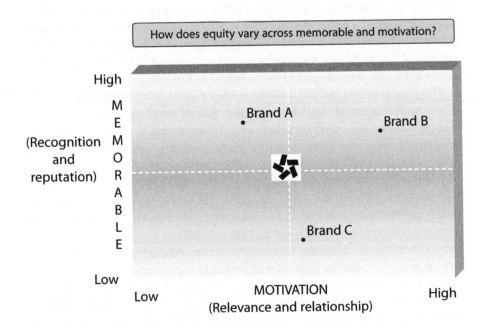

Figure 5.9 Brand vitality 3

today. If we went on to look at momentum, we would probably guess that the brand was weak on both rejuvenation and recruitment (although this might not necessarily be the case).

The beauty of brand vitality lies in its actionability. It allows you to set KPIs both for overall vitality/equity scores and for specific measures. This is important – the brand manager who is told to improve vitality next year might reasonably want some guidance on which levers he or she should pull to do this. Using the model of brand vitality, the manager could be told, for example, to focus on improving the motivation scores with particular attention to the relationship scores within that.

But to ensure that scores on those measures really do improve, the brand manager will need to consult a GAME Plan.

4. GAME PLANS

Sorry, this is not about Snakes and Ladders or Cluedo. The GAME in GAME plan stands for Goals, Actions, Measurement and Evaluation. The idea is to capture the connection between strategy and implementation, and it's a version of the simple template used by businesses like Procter and Pepsi known as OGSM (Objectives, Goals, Strategies and Measures). I liked it the first time I saw it, but thought it lacked a snappy name and felt the headings were tautological – hence GAME plan. The great thing about the GAME plan is that it is a summary which can be kept on one piece of paper, which all the key people in the business can refer to and understand – the CEO, marketing director, finance director and brand manager alike.

The example in Figure 5.10 shows what a GAME plan might look like for a 'wealth management' business – an area that all the major banks and financial institutions are currently piling into. It starts with the strategic idea for growth – in this case to become the leading wealth management brand for affluent business professionals. This is then translated into five goals (yes just five, never three or ten) which are listed in the left hand column. Next, come the specific actions in the marketing plan that will achieve those goals, and finally the factors to measure and evaluate their success. The linkages between all three columns should be clear and the methods of measurement and evaluation should be quantifiable wherever possible, although some qualitative or soft measurement and judgement will probably be required.

The board of a company like a GAME plan because they can have just one piece of paper which tells them exactly what's happening and where the brand should be going. When one of them bumps into the brand manager, rather than just saying, 'How's it going?' he or she knows precisely what questions to ask

OVERALL STRATEGIC VISION

To be the leading international wealth management brand among high nett worth business professionals (new vs old money) with a reputation of superior market insight and efficiency

Goals	Actions	Measurement and evaluation
1 Superior spontaneous awareness	• Relaunch brand identity • Identify and secure one major, relevant sponsorship property	• Increase 'first mention' from 10% to 50% in target group by year 2

2 Own 'market insight and efficiency' as key differentiators	• Relaunch internal KPIs to improve visible delivery
	• Improve and publicise market insight tools
	• New 360° communications
		• Internal audit (action standards to be agreed)
		• Brand tracking (by year 1)
		  – Raise 'is different' from 20% to 75%
		  – Achieve 50% awareness of both key attributes among 'aware' and 'would' consider

3 Highest cross-purchase of key wealth management services (banking, investment, protection)	• Develop new service offering integrated investment and insurance • Improve relationship management and cross purchase incentives	• Increase cross purchase from 1.5 services to 3+ by year 2 • More than 30% of business to come from new services by year 3
4 Dominate new market entrants	• Improve targeting tools • Devise new business and customer retention programmes	• 35% market share in 'younger' customer group by year 2 • Less than 5% customer attrition on-going
5 Expand into two new major market territories	• Evaluate options and make selection • Prepare new business case and entry selection	• 25% of total profit by year 3 to come from new geographic markets

Figure 5.10 GAME plan

and how to appraise the answers. The GAME plan makes life easier for brand managers, too, because it clarifies their goals and provides them with a clear yardstick to judge whether they are doing a good job or not. Its simplicity also means that it's easy to be flexible, because the framework within which change can occur is already clearly in place.

Having selected your KPIs, assessed your brand's health, dynamics and vitality and put the information together in a brief incisive GAME plan, you still need to answer one more all-important question. How much is that precious brand of yours really worth?

5. BRAND VALUATION

Thankfully for the marketer, the answer to the question 'How much is a brand worth?' is usually very, very satisfying. Even the quickest glance at the valuation of the world's top ten brands proves just how staggeringly valuable they really are.

	Brand	2001 Brand value (SMM)
1.	Coca-Cola	68 945
2.	Microsoft	65 068
3.	IBM	52 762
4.	GE	42 396
5.	Nokia	35 035
6.	Intel	34 665
7.	Disney	32 591
8.	Ford	30 092
9.	McDonald's	25 289
10.	AT&T	22 828

Figure 5.11 Estimated value of some leading brands

The problem for marketers is that these 'staggeringly valuable' assets don't appear on the balance sheet, although a consensus is building that perhaps they should. Indeed, according to *Accountancy Age* most City analysts would prefer it that way:

More than half the City analysts in the UK believe all internally generated intangible assets should be capitalised on a company balance sheet, according to a survey. It also reveals that 76 per cent of 800 analysts questioned say that more information on brand values is needed. The strong demand suggests that the City... accepts demands to see brand information in published accounts.

Accountancy Age, 28 June 2001

But if they are to appear on the balance sheet, there needs to be general agreement about how exactly they should be valued. Over recent years there's been a lot of debate about this, although there's still no one method of doing it that is approved by auditors. I was certainly very cynical for a long time. Respect to Interbrand for their championing of this issue and admiration for their reputation, but it always concerned me that a) there was so much subjectivity and arbitrariness in the methodology and b) it was of so little use to a marketer who wanted to understand what to change and how to create growth.

One way of looking at this is to say that the true value of a brand is its ability to command a price premium for a given volume of sales, or a higher volume of sales for a given price. There is obviously real value here, as this price premium will continue for a surprisingly long time even if no further money is invested in the brand, simply because fame in itself is a rare and precious commodity. But clearly any method of valuing brands also needs to take account of the forces of supply and demand – that, after all, is the way that most prices are determined. So perhaps we could also say that the ultimate value of a brand is simply how much others will pay to get their hands on it. Certainly, if you were the owner of the only widely recognised brand in a market, you would expect it to be more valuable than if it were one of two or three brands competing for the same customers. You would also expect a growing brand to be more valuable than one that was static or in decline.

This sense of market dynamics must be built into any brand valuation model if it is to have the credibility to win over the hard-nosed financial people who pull the strings in most companies. And these are the people, I repeat, that marketers need to address. For too long marketers and financiers have been speaking different business dialects, communicating more by gesture and sign than through mutual and subtle understanding. Marketers are supposed to be able to communicate with anyone – so it would seem sensible to start off by demonstrating these skills to the people who control our budgets. Only then can marketers think about reclaiming their rightful place in the life of a company – as the alchemists at the heart of the business process, magically conjuring gold from five simple base metals: Insight, Ideas, Innovation, Impact and, of course, Investment return.

THE STUFF THAT GETS IN THE WAY OF INVESTMENT RETURN

1. Resistance to change

If the strategy changes, then the measures must change. If 'what gets measured gets done', it follows that to do new things means you have to measure new things.

2. No truly connected balanced scorecard

It is difficult to get a business to focus on a set of measures on a balanced scorecard. More to the point, it's very difficult to wean them off the dominant measures of sales and profit because it is what most chairmen care about at the end of the day, and this communicates itself osmotically throughout the organisation. A balanced scorecard is made easier if people can see a simple set of measures or KPIs that connect. As part of the 'Grow Guinness' strategy, Guinness introduced a new set of measures called the 'Four As': aware, admire, adopt, advocate. It was based on its understanding of how people came be to be devotees of the brand with high consumption. You start with awareness and then move to 'admiration' – to persevere with this very bitter beer you have to genuinely want to be a Guinness drinker. This could be tracked on image scores. 'Adopt' is the trial stage and 'advocate' is the point where you become a regular drinker and actually start to evangelise the brand. The model was based on research and it made sense because it connected. Most balanced scorecards do not make sense because insufficient effort is put into understanding how they connect.

3. The KPIs aren't marketed

KPIs, and particularly new KPIs, have to be marketed within the business. This means planned and sustained communication. Personally, I am a big fan of notice boards in the foyer or canteen. Most companies these days seem to exhibit their share price, which for 99 per cent of the people who walk past it, is a measure they feel they can do very little about. It should be the KPIs up there in lights.

4. Lack of senior sponsorship

The attitudes and behaviour of the whole senior team are crucial to the effective communication of KPIs and the commitment that they generate. If the senior team understand the measures and use them – for example, by making it the first question they ask in meetings – then actions are connected to changes in the measures. At this point, the new KPIs will get awareness, admiration, adoption and advocacy.

5. Marketing and finance don't speak the same language

How do you learn a foreign language? Go to a few classes but then spend all your time with your English mates and never give yourself the chance to use the new language? This is what happens in most businesses when it comes to marketers learning finance and financial people learning marketing. You go on a course, learn all about balance sheets, P& L, cash flows and DCF yields, then you back to your marketing job and never use them. This happened to me at least three times in Unilever. It wasn't until I was running my own business that the stuff I had learnt started to make sense. I would not claim to be the most adept financial manager, but I can understand and speak the language. A company with marketers who really understand and use financial language and tools and vice versa is a company that will make the connection between marketing and investment return.

And another thing ...

In the old days, alchemy was certainly not a calling for the faint-hearted. Many alchemists were financially ruined by their relentless pursuit of gold; others poisoned themselves or went insane after inhaling the noxious gases produced by their experiments. But with the advent of the printing press, some alchemists saw a new and perhaps more lucrative outlet for the talents – instead of practising alchemy, they'd write books about it.

One such alchemist-turned-author was the Italian, John Aurelio Augurello, who had a keen understanding of the value of publicity and so sent a copy of his alchemical treatise to Pope Leo X in the hope of receiving some kind of financial favour or, at the very least, a papal puff for the back cover. His spirits were high when he was summoned to the Vatican and received by His Holiness himself. At the end of his audience, with great ceremony, the Pope presented him with a large purse. But as the penniless alchemist weighed it in his hand, he realised that it was completely empty. He stared at the Pope, open mouthed, wondering what it could mean.

'As you're such a great magician,' the Pope told him, with a smile, 'I thought you'd need something to keep all your gold in.'

In business today, filling that purse with gold is the job of the marketing alchemist – and his chances of success are considerably higher than were those of poor Augurello. Indeed, I promised at the start of this book that the alchemical process of the Five 'I's was an infallible method for producing marketing gold. It's certainly a process that enables you to draw on all the resources, skills and knowledge of a company and allows them to work together to produce the one clear goal of any commercial enterprise: top-line growth. But the process also requires marketers to rethink their relationships with their collaborators and colleagues. Modern marketers should be as comfortable in the board room as they are at the product launch. They should be as fluent in the language of finance as they are in the dialects of advertising, design or branding. Marketing, as we've seen, is a 360 degree activity which requires attention to every aspect of business, from the quality of insights gained in the research lab to the way that a used package gets thrown out with the trash.

But can I really claim that the Five 'I's is an infallible process? Well, if you follow it to the letter, I guarantee your success – or at least I would, if it weren't for all the stuff that gets in the way.

Decoding competitive propositions: a semiotic alternative to traditional advertising research

Michael Harvey, Guinness UDV

Malcolm Evans, Added Value

1. INTRODUCTION

This paper shows how innovative thinking and good client/agency communication can turn perspectives drawn from an unconventional knowledge domain to real competitive advantage. It outlines a project in which Guinness and a specialist team from Added Value used semiotics (the study of how any sign system – e.g. words, pictures, music, myth – creates meanings and evokes feelings), to develop a friendly analytical tool now used by Guinness worldwide to gain a new depth of insight into the competitive environment.

This system, the Competitor Advertising Decoding Kit, guides Guinness's marketers and planners in the analysis of likely consumer take-outs from current competitive ads, and helps them to decipher for each competitor the proposition that could ultimately drive these take-outs. By then mapping competitor advertising propositions, Guinness marketing and planning teams get a much clearer picture of the marketplaces they are operating in – and some of the main challenges and opportunities that face their brands.

2. CLIENT STARTING POINT – GUINNESS

In 1998 Guinness created a new process to develop brand propositions. This process required an understanding of four key elements in order to create the best proposition for the brand anywhere in the world:

- marketing objectives (to ensure the proposition was 'fit for purpose')
- consumer needs and motivations (to ensure the proposition was motivating)
- product attributes/perceptions (to ensure a credible proposition)
- knowledge of competitive advertising propositions (to ensure a distinctive proposition).

There was nothing particularly earth-shattering here, just good practice rigorously applied. But Guinness discovered that while it invariably knew a great deal about the first three elements, it rarely knew much about competitive propositions. This gap was clearly important, and Guinness acknowledged that a core understanding of competitive positionings (from a consumer perspective) was essential to maintain its own distinctive positioning in the marketplace.

To gain this knowledge it was considered too extravagant to commission a special study in every market of exactly what positioning consumers attributed to other brands (and existing conventional U&A's did not give the richness of response needed). So data was patchy, largely from ad hoc qualitative studies, and often out of date. What Guinness wanted was a fast cost-effective solution.

The first breakthrough came with a conceptual flip: from the idea of researching consumer response to the idea of directly analysing the advertising stimulus itself as a potential solution to the challenge of understanding competitive propositions.

This is where specialist semiotic analysis of brand communications presented itself as a possible solution. In the client's mind was a web of sometimes conflicting thoughts and associations. Among this were recollections of a French colleague at an advertising agency back in the 1980s, claiming that semiotics is a door you can use to open up any company's advertising and get access to its knowledge about how to motivate consumers. Do that for all the competition and you learn everything there is to know about your marketplace.

But then there is all the confusing jargon that goes with semiotics – paradigms, metaphors, metonyms, and what have you. There was a story around at the time about a fairly typical presentation by a French semiologist to a straight up, no nonsense American pet food client on innovation in premium food for small dogs. Two hours of technical terminology and deep cultural analysis culminating in the *coup de grace*: 'And so we see, the dog is not a dog at all. The dog is a cat.'

The client responds (names have been changed here to protect the innocent): 'Jean-Claude the dog is NOT a fuckin' cat. The dog is a fuckin' dog.'

Then some direct personal experience with semiotics (again pre-Guinness) and in the spirits market. The client company on that occasion needed a worldwide model for how people choose between alcoholic drinks. The qualitative research costing came out at £650K (this was in 1989) and the semiotics came out at £60K. The client opted for the semiotics. For that price they did, eventually, get what they were looking for. But it was a struggle to dig out and rework the one key matrix from a mass of theoretical background noise and relatively unhelpful detail.

So semiotics, in summary and from the buyer's point of view, covers a spectrum:

Magic<————————>Mystification

Where you come out as a client (prospective or actual) is likely to depend on what you have heard and the people you have worked with – some at either extreme, others somewhere in the middle.

The real need in this case of this project, then, was for an instant, affordable way for Guinness marketers anywhere in the world to understand all competitors' positionings (as projected by advertising) from a consumer perspective at exactly the point in the process when a new Guinness proposition was being prepared. A tough brief for any agency! In the event it was the Decoder team, Added Value's semiotic specialists, who came up with the most promising ideas for a solution.

3. SEMIOTIC STARTING POINT – DECODER

'Semiotically, semiotics does itself no favours.' So speaks *Guardian* columnist and innovation guru Guy Browning on a communications methodology that has had some communication problems of its own. This heritage (and the need to move on from it) is why people buying Added Value's Decoder often do not realise that what they are buying is semiotics. The technicalities are deliberately kept out of view (unless clients specifically ask to look inside the methodology). Decoder is stealth semiotics.

What does this accessible/plain English version of semiotics normally deliver?

- Cultural understanding for market entry and cross-cultural communications platforms designed to work with the highest common factors across markets. (Such as understanding the most motivating emergent meanings of, say, indulgence across Europe today. Which will work best for your brand? What is the most appropriate cross-cultural 'language' of indulgence – verbal, visual, design, musical cues or whatever? How is this language evolving – what is the current pace and direction of change in the cues used to communicate indulgence?)

- Understanding the communication codes (or 'unwritten rules') of your category. Which codes are being used (or broken) by your brand and the competition and to what effect? Understand competitors in context (evolving category codes and popular culture) – better than they understand themselves. Understand where you should be going in communications terms (e.g. in advertising, packaging or website design), and how to get there.
- Broader vision and deeper consumer insight. Where qualitative research tends to play back consumer norms of today, semiotic analysis develops a more visionary perspective on where culture and communications may be leading us.

This is head-above-the-parapet research, creating a more informed context in which we can talk to consumers direct and come up with visionary perspectives that allow brands to lead the evolution of their marketplace rather than just react to mainstream public opinion.

From the agency point of view, excitement about the Guinness brief came from two main sources. First was the opportunity to work with the pioneering brand in innovative and culturally salient advertising – past and present, outstanding in the context of not just beer but advertising in general.

Equally important was the challenge to take semiotics another step on from theory and the academic world, not only by demonstrating its power in decoding competitive advertising, but also by doing this in a transparent and accessible way: so much so that the analysis would model a tool that Guinness marketing and planning teams could then go on to use for themselves to continuously update their knowledge base on competitive advertising. The brief itself ensured that comprehensible, hands-on semiotics was not only a nice-to-have but the main goal, the object of the whole exercise.

4. GROUNDWORK – THE INTERNATIONAL LANGUAGE OF BEER

Decoder was tasked with devising a clear process to allow Guinness marketers anywhere in the world (after a brief period of training) to work out exactly what proposition consumers were likely to be taking out of a brand's advertising, as a major step on the way to understanding the brand's overall positioning from the consumer's point of view.

To start creating this Competitor Advertising Decoding Kit, key beer brands' advertising was sourced from six representative markets world wide:

Cameroon, Germany, Malaysia, Spain, the UK and the United States, and analysed by semiologists with expert knowledge of these markets.

After analysing the relevant TV reel and print ads, each analyst mapped out the beer codes characteristic of his/her market, then analysed advertising for the major brands in terms of codes deployed, codes challenged or explicitly broken, and the overall profile of codes used by each brand – residual (dated advertising styles and conventions), dominant (middle of the road for today), or emergent (dynamic, innovative). Then the country analyst made a hypothetical assessment of core consumer takeout from each brand's advertising before translating this into the language of advertising propositions, incorporating the relative weighting in the ads of three key benefit sources: product attributes (What?); user imagery (Who?) and consumer need (Why?). The final step was to map the brands' advertising propositions along axes spontaneously suggested by the category codes coming out of the analysis – the conceptual and emotional 'world' of beer advertising in that particular market.

Illustrating part of this process, Figure A1.1 shows some summary outputs for two key brands examined in the UK.

The merger of all the national data gave us, first of all, a verbal and visual snapshot of the cultural meaning of beer globally (defined against wine and spirits) – part of the basic 'cultural software' any alien landing on planet Earth would need to get hold of to become plausibly one of us.

More critically, for the Decoding Kit that eventually evolved from this research, the combined analysis gave us a map of the international language of beer – the full repertoire of global beer advertising codes.

What is a code? Think about the following bits of communication in isolation from each other:

- a crashing wave
- the sound of a cap coming off a bottle (Psssst!)
- back-lit golden liquid with bubbles moving up
- a drop of condensation sliding down a glass
- drop sliding down an ice-frosted bottle
- thirst (sun, parched land, water)
- intense physical activity
- representations of thirsty people
- the first big glug, subsequent release of breath and spontaneous sound of satisfaction
- energy burst.

A code is what makes all these hang together in our minds, and starts each of us extending that list, filling the gaps using the cultural software we have acquired

Carling Black Label	Stella Artois
Key codes heritage/roots beer enjoyment irreverent masculinity sporting achievement	**Key codes** parody humour heritage beer enjoyment
Brand specific execution **of codes** nationalism; 'Rule Britannia' (Dambusters, Union Jacks, 'best-selling beer in Britain') strength (4.1%) tabloid attitude Carling Premiership	**Brand specific execution** **of codes** French language music cinematic references idyllic France 'reassuringly expensive'
Proposition source Why: Belonging What: Strength Who: Lad user	**Proposition source** What: Best ingredients = best beer Who: Discerning drinker (Why: Personal indulgence)
Substantiators brewed to 4.1% football sponsorship patriotism popularity	**Substantiators** premium (reassuringly expensive)
Advertising proposition **(hypothesis)** My Carling confirms me as one of the lads.	**Advertising proposition** **(hypothesis)** Stella Artois is the ultimate reward.

Figure A1.1 Semiotic analysis of UK beer advertising: some summary outputs

as members of a culture and consumers of advertising. These are all signifiers held together by the idea of refreshment (no less than red, green and amber lights are all held together by an underlying 'grammar' of traffic regulation).

If you are an alien you may be able to view these signifiers in isolation from each other. As a paid-up member of human consumer culture you should find it impossible. You should also be reaching already for the metaphorical extensions of physical refreshment into attitude, state of mind, youthfulness, no bullshit and so on.

It's all part of the programme, as sure as when you are channel surfing you will spot the cues that say news, soap, sitcom, documentary, car ad, snacks ad within a split second, in the same way that most two-year-olds can now, almost instinctively, identify the Coke logo or McDonald's arches from a small fragment of the complete image.

The international language of beer, the Decoder analysts concluded, can ultimately be focused down into refreshment plus 25 other key communication codes. The 26 codes map out into 7 clusters. Something like this map should, with minor variations, be arrived at by any team of semiologists who set out to analyse a good sample of worldwide beer advertising. Since it remains a key component of the Competitor Advertising Decoding Kit – which has only been in use so far for a year or so and, we believe, gives Guinness real competitive advantage – we will only reveal some parts of it here (see Figure A1.2).

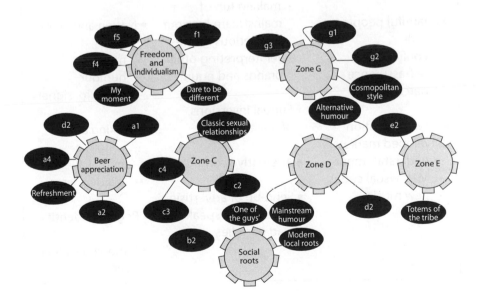

Figure A1.2 International language of beer advertising: outline structure of the code map

The codes towards the left and the bottom of the map express the drinker/product relationship and social roots – where the drinker feels a sense of origin and belonging. The codes to the right capture characteristically beer-oriented images of bonding, sociability and humour. Towards the top of the map we have outer- and inner-directed expressions of aspiration, a sense of where I want to be going (rather than where I'm coming from).

Each of the codes coming out of the semiotic analysis, as in the case of refreshment above, is a set of signifiers or communication cues held together by a core idea (see Figure A1.3 for some other examples).

Cosmopolitan style	Alternative humour	Totems of the tribe
• Modern city life – style bars – bright lights, big city – market savvy • Western (vs local) clothing and lifestyle – Western music – Western attitude • Beautiful people – style – confidence, self-assurance – narcissism • New generation (developed markets) – understatement – MTV visual codes – new music – irony	• Self-deprecating humour – twist in the tail • Irony, cynicism – defining style clans and sub-cultures • Parody – making fun of mainstream humour and 'serious' genres – reinterpreting other brands and equities • Surreal inversions of reality • Alternative comedians • Send-up of advertising – marketing speak – ad parodies	• Bonding focal points – dances, music – teams – couples, family – hobbyists • Workplace and after work • Nation and icons – flags – music – humour – funny foreigners • Looking alike – uniforms – animal allegory – lizards, frogs • Regional identity • National/regional beer

Figure A1.3 International Language of Beer Advertising: signifiers for three other sample codes

At this point both agency and client felt that we had a good grasp, in an international context, of how beer advertising communicates and the underlying propositions competitor brands are conveying to consumers. The main challenge, however, still lay ahead – how to repackage what the Decoder team has learnt about beer advertising and about their own analytical processes into a tool that Guinness people world-wide could now go on to use for themselves in decoding competitive propositions.

5. THE COMPETITOR ADVERTISING DECODING KIT

Between this groundwork (debriefed in July 1998) and the final launch of the Decoding Kit in September 1999 there was a year of prototyping, revising, communicating problems and issues – and listening. Some key learnings came out of this process:

- Semiotics isn't rocket science. On the contrary, it's the common sense of the future. As we recognise increasingly the role of communications and culture in structuring our perceptions, behaviour, even our sense of our own identity, so we have to become more code-adept and media literate. Younger consumers are already masters (and mistresses) of instinctive semiotics – interacting with the work of advertising creatives and continuously upping the stakes of innovation, subtlety, irony and cross-reference. They are the semiotic pioneers. As William Gibson says, 'The future is already here; it's just not very well distributed yet.'
- Semiotics is most valuable in helping us move into this future when it doesn't wrap itself in jargon (or conventional consultancy's trademark pitfalls of narcissism and spin).
- An expert is someone who has forgotten the rules. So you will find it very difficult to communicate to others how you do what you do by introspecting on yourself doing it. In this respect, communicating knowledge is probably a bit like making love to a beautiful woman (or man, for that matter). When the Decoder team, to develop the analytical tool for Guinness, retraced its steps in analysing the language of beer advertising and getting to the individual brand propositions, it was the marketers on the team who were best able to translate what the semiologists were doing into accessible rules. Conversely the semiologists, by interrogating the marketers, were able to help deduce the unspoken protocols for formulating advertising propositions.

So what is the Competitor Advertising Decoding Kit that finally emerged, and how does it work?

The purpose of the tool, as stated upfront, is to help its users gain a better understanding of what competitors are communicating in their ads. It does so by guiding the development of informed hypotheses on the core consumer takeout and underlying advertising proposition in samples of current competitive advertising. The tool adopts the working assumption that the underlying advertising proposition expresses the key brand benefit, and that this benefit, in the world of current beer advertising, will be based in one of three areas – product attribute (e.g. smooth, creamy taste), user imagery (e.g. individuals who don't conform to the norm) or human needs (e.g. gives you a sense of belonging).

In practice, Guinness marketers use the tool when developing a new advertising proposition for a Guinness brand, at which time an understanding of competitive advertising propositions is critical, or when a competitor launches a new campaign, to understand their new proposition and the implications for Guinness brands. Otherwise it is also used as part of the annual planning cycle, when Guinness local market teams review all competitive advertising.

The system works by guiding teams of two or three people through an analysis of current campaigns for competitive brands. Each local market team, ideally, includes one marketer/consumer planner experienced in the beer market, another who is more in touch with young adult culture, and a third person who is a non-marketer – such as a sales person more in touch with the trade environment. The team is taken through a two-stage process (see Figure A1.4).

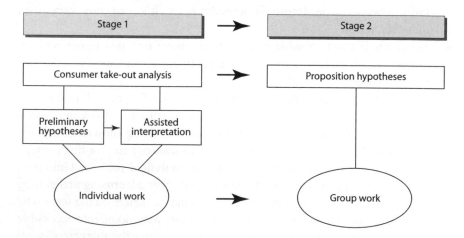

Figure A1.4 Process chart from Competitor Advertising Decoding Kit handbook

Stage 1: Consumer take-out analysis

The key breakthrough in moving ahead from the original groundwork here was in understanding that interpretation (which experts do spontaneously, firing on all cylinders at once) needs to be broken down into component parts.

Here the Guinness team members work individually, each looking at examples of current advertising for two or three competitive brands. The objective at this stage is to think deeply about the advertising and pay attention to detail, blocking the natural temptation to jump to conclusions too soon, also suspending any specialist marketing knowledge and going 'through the looking glass' to adopt the consumer's point of view.

At this stage the system first prompts the user to think separately about executional details along 12 different dimensions of the advertising – including the people (celebrities, consumer types, who they are meant to appeal to, what they tell us about the brand), genre (realism, fantasy, surrealism, abstraction), music (styles of music used and their associations in popular culture), colours (which ones predominate, what they are communicating).

The aim here is to take the time to deconstruct a brand's advertising, to dig into all its richness and become conscious of a palette of creative stimuli that may, in many cases, be working on consumers below the level of consciousness.

Once the advertising for a particular brand has been deconstructed, the next stage of guided analysis is to arrange the material gathered from the ads in a hierarchy and funnel it all down to the essentials – the key ideas and feelings being communicated: for example, the implied target and the area in which key brand benefits, on a preliminary assessment, appear to be operating.

The code cards

At this point in the process the user will view the ads for this brand again, review the preliminary hypotheses on consumer take-out, and enter a phase of assisted interpretation using the code cards supplied as part of the Decoding Kit. The key breakthrough in moving on from the original groundwork here was to transform and streamline the original International Language of Beer Advertising map (Figure A1.2) into a more user-friendly tool. This is a pack of themed cards designed and produced by the Brown KSDP design agency. The cards are something like a cross between Tarot and analytical mini-mood boards, capturing 21 major codes of global beer advertising (slimmed down from the original analysis's 26).

As well as enriching the user's broad understanding of the underlying 'language' of beer (images, words, music and so on), the code cards serve an immediate practical function in understanding likely consumer take-out from specific ads and campaigns.

So the marketer using the Decoding Kit can review the themes printed on the card backs (one theme per card) and when he or she encounters one that matches something in the preliminary analysis of likely consumer take-out, flip over the card in question to test the interpretation against the communication cues reproduced on front of the card (words, images, music, personalities) that are normally used to communicate this theme.

Conversely a quick scan of the words and images on the front of the cards will allow users of the system to spot any features of the competitive ads that they have had difficulty interpreting, and flip the relevant card over to spot the idea or theme these cues normally communicate in beer ads.

The review of ads against the code cards and subsequent centring/focusing of thoughts on likely consumer take-out completes Stage 1 of the analysis of a competitive brand's advertising. When each member has completed this part of the process for his or her assigned competitive brands, the whole team gets together in Stage 2 to review the individual data and work out the likely propositions driving the ads that result in these consumer take-outs.

Stage 2: Proposition hypotheses

Here the Stage 1 learning is shared amongst the team, the main messages and consumer take-outs for competitive advertising agreed, and these findings translated into advertising propositions for each of the competitors analysed in the market. The Stage 2 process follows key steps for each competitor:

1. Begin to develop the proposition by pulling out the key benefit-driven proposition sources (product attribute, user imagery, human need), revisiting the preliminary work done on this in Stage 1.
2. Rank these potential proposition sources in order to identify the key driver behind the brand's advertising, that is, the clearest, most motivating consumer benefit (what the brand is doing for the drinker).
3. From the detailed analysis of the ads, assess the supports being asserted or demonstrated for this proposition (why should consumers believe it?).
4. Draft the likely proposition (core benefit is ...) and supports (... because ...).
5. Finally assess the competitive proposition against a checklist of six key success criteria including relevance to target and distinctiveness in the marketplace.

6. THE DECODING KIT IN ACTION

At the final pre-launch trial of the Decoding Kit in the summer of 1999, an international Guinness team looked at some current UK TV ads for Fosters ('He who drinks Australian thinks Australian' – the French execution where a man helps a woman re-stack her shopping; the German on the telephone asking his kidnapped wife where his golf clubs are; and the Italian trouser-maker making a rapid exit from a family gathering before being kissed by the godfather).

The Stage 1 consumer take-out analysis focused on a number of key themes including Australian-ness, 'real man' machismo, putting down women, an implied drinker who puts his sense of masculinity before anything else, irony and visual/cinematic sophistication (what felt like snippets of classical film genres, possible visual quotes from actual films of the late 1970s and 1980s).

A review of the code cards confirmed some of the spontaneous analysis (regular guys, mainstream humour, classic sexual relationships) but also cued elements of new thinking into the analysis – particularly around refreshment (and how literal refreshment is also communicated metaphorically via attitude, fresh humour etc.) and modern local culture, a code that offers a vicarious kind of rootedness, authenticity and belonging (how we can all now be virtually Australian, Irish, American, Jamaican or whatever, and what the various permutations of co-opted identity signify emotionally).

The proposition hypotheses stage of the analysis addressed product attribute (refreshing), user imagery (refreshing attitude and humour, the Australian male) and human need (feeling masculine) before focusing in on user imagery as the most likely core of the consumer take-out. The first shot at translating this into a likely advertising proposition was something along the lines of 'Drinking Fosters shows what a refreshingly real man you are', with the irreverent Australian attitude as a key component in delivering this proposition.

The immediate reaction to the Decoding Kit was that it definitely worked. Fosters provided an example of fairly straightforward advertising, so in this case the code cards did not have a major role to play in helping decode a complex or potentially obscure meaning. However, even in a relatively straightforward case such as this, a process that facilitates discussion and insists on attention to detail and evaluation of alternative paths of interpretation or prioritisation establishes a mind-set in which people think systematically about what competitors are doing and avoid jumping to conclusions too quickly. Straplines, for example, are rarely if ever used to communicate an advertising proposition directly.

Coincidentally, a chance encounter with someone from the advertising agency shortly after this trial run brought some independent corroboration of the Fosters advertising proposition: a slightly hazy recollection, but something like 'Being a Fosters drinker gives you access to a positive laid-back attitude' (with Australian-ness, again, obviously a key supporting idea).

The emphasis may be a bit different but the two versions of the proposition are clearly occupying the same cultural terrain. And the Decoding Kit comes complete with a warning that users should not expect to have decoded the precise wording of the actual competitive advertising proposition every time. In an imperfect world, advertising rarely communicates perfectly what it is intended to communicate to consumers.

This imperfection may, however, be viewed as a strength of the Decoding Kit rather than a weakness. Alluring as it may seem at first glance to have a window into the intentions or 'mind' of the competitive brand via the advertising, it is, ultimately, more conducive to real competitive advantage to view the advertising as a mirror – and gain real insight into what consumers see reflected there.

So the hypothetical competitive advertising proposition, produced by a kind of reverse engineering from likely consumer take-out, is more useful in terms of understanding and mapping out the marketplace than would be access to the actual propositions driving competitive ads. Thus the Decoding Kit brings to Guinness marketers on a day to day basis one of the key benefits of specialist semiotic analysis – the advantage, in many cases, of understanding competitive brands and what they communicate better than the competitors themselves do.

7. CURRENT STATE OF PLAY

The Competitor Advertising Decoding Kit has now been distributed throughout the Guinness world, and has added a new rigour to brand proposition development. Using the kit, two or three Guinness marketers working together for half a day produce analyses far more sophisticated than the old advertising agency 'Competitive Review', which concentrated on content or likeability rather than any significant insight into what goes on in consumers' heads about the positioning of brands. The findings of this ongoing work may not be as accurate or robust as full-blown advertising research, but they are fit for purpose and highly cost-effective.

From the agency point of view, methodological information shared and made more accessible has been learning gained. The semiotic approach behind the International Language of Beer Advertising map and the code cards (identifying the components and structure of this communication 'genre') can be applied to advertising in any other category – or any other medium in a brand's communications mix (for example the codes of packaging, websites, POS, retail outlet design, sponsorship, direct mail). A major buzz for the Decoder team arrived with the dawning grasp of this principle – and the potential extension of this work on beer and advertising to the quest for competitive advantage in other categories (automotive, financial services, food, pharmaceuticals, telecoms, IT, personal care, household and so on), to other elements of the brand mix, and to the relationship between these different components of communication.

There has also been some fascinating incidental learning on the world of beer advertising and the differences between markets:

- German beer ads, for example, are mostly about authenticity, heritage, purity, implied national superiority and exclusivity. Beer is allowed to communicate cultural signifiers of German-ness that have been taboo in mainstream political discourse since 1945.
- UK beer advertising, in contrast, is centred very much in the area of bonding and humour – particularly in the irony and wacky surrealism that is wedded to the fading culture of laddism. Whassup?, all the rage one day then played out the next – a symptom of this advertising style's current decline.
- Party and fiesta codes around beer in Spain and Latin America – serving the role played by humour in expressing bonding and emotional release in other markets (and drawing beer codes closer to those of soft drinks).
- Beer drinking as overt aspiration and badging (as in the cosmopolitan culture code) are characteristics of beer advertising mainly in developing markets, where beer in general and/or international brands in particular come to signify modernity and sophistication (compared with local brews).
- In UK and United States new trends filter in via inner-directed values (individualism, freedom) rather than outer-directed (overt badging, display). 'Cool' is essentially what can't be defined, captured, copied. When your dad says things are 'cool' they're not cool any more (not even the word 'cool'). So inner directed is the new outer directed in code and media-savvy markets.

8. CONCLUSIONS (PROVISIONAL)

For anyone who has not previously heard of semiotics, Guinness's Competitor Advertising Decoding Kit is a good introduction to a discipline that helps unlock the power of culture and communications in shaping consumer perceptions and behaviour today. For anyone who has heard of semiotics, the system may come as a surprise – moving its application to marketing and research on from a hitherto niche, specialist, sometimes obscure form of analysis towards greater transparency, relevance and interactivity.

This is only the beginning. The spirit of experiment and collaboration is starting to spin off its own unpredictable offspring.

Guinness recently briefed a team of UK marketers and planners to decode examples of Japanese beer advertising, using the kit and English translations of the language. These were assessed against readings produced locally by a Japanese team. The result was around 80 per cent accuracy in the UK assessment, with the 20 per cent of understanding lost mainly through a failure to recognise the meanings and associations circulating around Japanese celebrities used in the ads. If semiotics can offer a cost saving against more conventional forms of research, what emerges here may begin to challenge some conventional semiotic assumptions (for example, that you need to be fully immersed in a language and culture to understand its communications). It all depends, of course, on what's fit for purpose, and on the trade-offs between relative certainty on the one hand and cost/speed/convenience on the other.

Another informal project currently in hand involves three teams looking at the Whassup? ads to evaluate their significance in terms of consumer insight: a Guinness team using the Decoding Kit; some semiotic experts (who have 'forgotten the rules'), and a mixed team of researchers and marketing people from outside both Guinness and Added Value (using their common sense without access either to the kit or to formal semiotic training). There are no assumptions or prejudgements about the findings. Whatever comes out will be fed into the development of the Guinness Decoding Kit and the next cycle of applied semiotic thinking within Added Value and Brown KSDP's Decoder methodology.

Other possibilities arise from the as yet untapped technological potential of a system like the Guinness Decoding Kit. Its physical design, in its current incarnation, is a key feature contributing to a user-friendliness and emotional warmth that the term 'semiotics' could never convey. Its conceptual content, however (rich in words, sounds, images and perpetually updating along with innovation in advertising codes), points ahead from the semiotics of Tarot, board games and instruction manuals to the world of on-line and multimedia. Watch this space …

Levi Strauss: a business in denial

Paul McGowan, Added Value

Flemming from Thygesen, Levi Strauss Europe

From the day Nick Kamen walked into a launderette in 1985 through to the mid-1990s, Levi Strauss & Co enjoyed unprecedented growth year after year, stimulated by the Original Jeans ad campaign, one of the best ad campaigns every tracked by Millward Brown.

Throughout this period the sole focus was on how to make 501® jeans look fresh and exciting every six months in the next ad campaign. Increasingly, the Levi's® brand became synonymous with the 501® jeans for (initially) good and for (increasingly) worse, as the steam began to go out of both the product and the brand.

As a company, Levi Strauss had settled comfortably into a work style where double digit growth on an annual basis became accepted as a natural state of affairs. Beating the sales plan was normal. 'Consumer insight' was the exclusive domain of a handful of designers, and product innovation was essentially expressed through new ways of communicating 501® jeans which represented in excess of 60 per cent of all sales in bottoms. Increasingly, we allowed our focus to wander away from consumers and the marketplace to internal supply chain issues and how to better reward ourselves for the great work we were achieving.

Because Levi Strauss had grown to expect success, the role of research became that of principal cheerleader: market share only went up, equity only improved, and in focus groups consumers always spoke in glowing terms about the brand. Inadvertently, we created a platform from which it became increasingly difficult to be critical of anything that the Levi's® brand did. Likewise, it reduced the role of the (small) research organisation to relatively passive information provision, which focused on the actual research process rather than on the application and usage of the consumer insights, which genuinely did reside within the information but went largely unexplored.

The research tools in place at the time, in line with the focus on the Original Jeans campaign as the primary driver of news and innovation, were largely focused on advertising. We had no research around either product or retail, two areas that would prove to be massive areas of weakness once the bottom fell out of the 501® jeans trend. Our main equity tracking tools were set up to only interview consumers who had bought jeans in the last six months. A 'great' idea in a stable market but a major barrier to understanding what is happening to your brand when the category goes into double digit decline and the competition comes from outside of jeans!

Essentially, research became 'due diligence'; we did it because we 'had to' not because we were committed to actually working with consumer insights.

By early 1997, there were clear indications that all was not well, but we chose to ignore them: the jeans market amongst young men (our core market) declined by 6 per cent, equity in Scandinavia (which was talked about as an opinion leading market) was in decline, a qualitative 501® jeans study showed that young consumers were beginning to sign out of 501® jeans.

ON THE VERGE OF A CRISIS

By the end of 1997 and fuelled by the downtrend, we started to pull the various strands of information together in a more structured manner to create a complete analysis of the consumer, market and brand situation across Europe. The picture wasn't pretty.

The jeans market was in free fall. Consumers were drifting to vertically integrated stores such as Zara, Mango, H&M, Gap and so on, and they were increasingly finding other garments than jeans to wear: combat pants, casual trousers, outdoor wear, high tech fibres etcetera. By the end of 1997, consumption of Levi's® jeans amongst young men and women had declined

	JEANS MARKET (MIO UNITS)			LEVI'S® CONSUMPTION (MIO UNITS)			SHARE OF LEVI'S® LOSS
	1997	2000	% shift	1997	2000	% shift	
Men 11+	143.4	134.7	−6.1%	18.5	13.5	−27.0%	−41.3%
11–24	48.0	39.5	−17.7%	9.4	5.2	−44.7%	−34.7%

	JEANS MARKET (MIO UNITS)			LEVI'S® CONSUMPTION (MIO UNITS)			SHARE OF LEVI'S® LOSS
	1997	2000	% shift	1997	2000	% shift	
Women 11+	132.0	116.9	−11.4%	12.9	5.8	−55.0%	−58.7%
11–24	47.3	32.8	−30.7%	9.2	2.8	−69.6%	−52.9%

Figure A2.1 The shrinking jeans market

by 6 per cent compared with the previous year. A number which was to get much worse as we'd go on to lose over 50 per cent of our consumption among young consumers between 1997 and 2000!

The way consumers talked about the Levi's® brand was increasingly distant. Just another fat American corporation: 'Levi's® is in a panic. They are losing share and are desperate to stay cool.' Product ubiquity and lack of innovation: '501® jeans fit every ass fabulously; unfortunately every ass wears one.'

Equity numbers, when we started to expand the scope of our study just a little to include designer jeans, declined dramatically. It was the first clear sign that we had been too narrow in our 'internal' view of the marketplace we were engaged in, and that as competition was toughening and moving forward, we were falling backwards fast by standing still.

The biggest internal challenge was how to overcome the business inertia and mentality that research only brings good news. The initial response to the situation analysis was one of 'What do you mean equity is down? You do know that the sales forecast is up, right?'

The fundamental choice from a research point of view was, how far does your responsibility extend? Is it to inform the business of the situation it is in and allow it to make a choice on how to act, or is it to compel it to act? In choosing the second route, we put our necks on the line. We continuously sought out a senior audience to pound home the message that, though we as a company expected more success from our current formula, the signs from

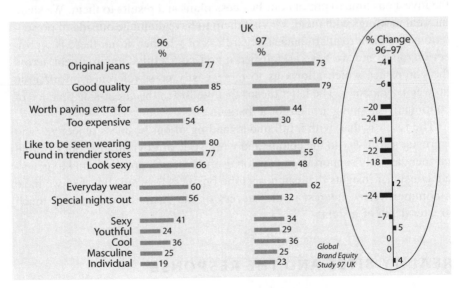

Figure A2.2 The introduction of CK jeans to the UK shows Levi's reposition as less premium, less sexy

consumers and the marketplace were that more of the same was a route that would quickly take us nowhere but backwards.

Taking a well thought through and firm position which went against company culture ultimately gave us an infinite amount of credibility when reality caught up with us and the sales forecast suddenly did go down. It created a platform that allowed a total overhaul of the research tools in our kit. More importantly it allowed a fundamental change in the way in which we engaged with the broader company, establishing us as partner with a stake in the actions taken.

To get into this position, and to respond when given the opening, placed specific requirements on the internal research team and on the way we engage with our outside partners. Internally, it required a shift in focus away from the research process itself, to the take-out from that process, to the actual usage. It meant thoroughly understanding the brand and business needs, often under-standing the needs better than the people officially employed to make the deci-sions. It meant being both willing and able to engage in a debate about what actions to take, and inspire colleagues to follow the path in which we believed, based on the consumer insight generated.

It fundamentally changed the way we had to work with our external part-ners. Many companies claim to want 'partnerships' with their research agen-cies. Most don't actually realise what it takes to achieve it. To allow us to shift our focus from the detail of the research process to the business application, it was essential to ensure partnership with our external agencies. To achieve this we invest our time to present our business plans and results to them. We share internal meetings with them, we visit them to have dialogue outside of presen-tations, we have regular contacts regardless of whether or not there is a proj-ect ongoing, and we have established a non-competitive environment across the companies which allows us to more easily cross-reference information between companies. The latter means that we forfeit the client-side practice of continually shopping around for a 'bargain'.

The result is that, with a full understanding of our business objectives and a greater sensitivity to the culture and work style of Levi Strauss, our external partner can truly support us to develop useful research programs and to gener-ate consumer insights that can propel the business forward. Because we have a common vested interest in the success of the business, we achieve much greater depth of insights.

REALITY BITES AND THE RESPONSE

By mid-1998 the message had finally been received and with the business now cognisant of the gravity of the situation, an internal turnaround team, working in partnership with Added Value, was given eight weeks to deliver a new brand vision. It started by taking a hard look at the fundamental pillars on which the brand and the business had been built over the preceding 12 years:

- In what market does Levi's® compete?
- Who is/are the core consumer target(s) and what are their key needs?
- What defines the enduring distinction of the Levi's® brand?
- What product line will most effectively deliver the brand for the target?

Big questions which required some fast thinking, sound judgement and authoritative answers. The situation analysis conducted in late 1997 gave the research function a respect and a voice that it had never previously been granted. From the outset it sat side by side with the brand team in shaping the process and making the calls that would ultimately define the new brand vision.

Market segmentation

The first of these questions may sound frighteningly obvious, but it was of vital significance. For years the company had defined itself as the leading jeans manufacturer in the denim jeans market. Right, and as it transpired, very, very wrong. Throughout 1997 the business continued to measure its own performance against that of the jeans category, and applauded itself on its ability to continue to grow against a category which was beginning to decline. Meanwhile, non-jeanswear was growing exponentially. To any casual observer, kids were taking off their jeans and donning their utility style khaki and combats. Share of jeans was still safe at this point but brand equity, sales volume and profit were falling away.

The answer was simple. The market was casual apparel, the broad collection of clothing alternatives from which younger consumers select, among other things, denim jeanswear: a simple but dramatic change to the key metrics the organisation would look at in judging its own performance and that of its newly identified competitors.

If that was the market, it was obviously a very big market within which distinct clusters of users, needs, occasions and products could be discerned and marketed to. The business needed to be clear that it was approaching the market in the way its consumers did. There was no time, budget or appetite for a first principles market segmentation study, but there was a wealth of internal knowledge and understanding of the market waiting to be focused and distilled down into a coherent model of market segmentation.

The process was straightforward: a two day Market Mapping™ workshop attended by the entire brand vision steering team, in which the dynamics of the casual apparel market were attacked from the five key doors (the Five 'W's) that can explain consumer choice in any market: the who (demographically and psychographically), the what (product), the when and the where (occasion), and the why (need).

Traditionally, the business had looked at the market from a who and a what perspective and in a very simple manner. There were 'cooler' consumers whom the business needed to nurture and there were more mainstream consumers who followed the lead taken by their 'cooler' cousins. And they all bought into the coolest jean, the Levi's® 501 jeans. Keep it cool at the top of the triangle and the rest will take care of itself: a standard trickle down model of adoption and influence.

The workshop looked very hard at occasion as a potentially more significant explanation of the choices consumers make, but ultimately concluded that the interaction between the who and the when was of crucial importance in making sense of the majority of the specific purchase decisions that happen in casual apparel: what you wear to go clubbing/vegetate on a Sunday morning/attend a lecture is best explained by who you wish to portray yourself as on that occasion. And within the who, it quickly became apparent that it was insufficient to make a simple cool/uncool cut. There were different kinds of cool kids who behaved and influenced the market in different ways, and equally there were different kinds of mainstream consumers whose attitudes and needs on specific occasions were clearly different. In total we got to six core consumer clusters.

Leading edge typologies

- Cultural Creatives: Generate new idea and trends. Free spirits who seek out undiscovered sources of inspiration. Largely unconcerned by the thoughts of others they plough their own creative furrow. Think Tracy Emin.
- Modernists: Seek status and success with an intelligent twist. Male/female aged 21–35, sociability is key for these networkers who live for the social whirl. Working in media or want to.
- The Edge: The most tribal of the groupings, they wear their insignia with pride – be it hip-hop or skate style. Integrity is all for this (mostly) male target.

Mainstream typologies

- Fast Fashion Flirts: Sassy, sparky and determined, these girls know how to have fun. Think Denise van Outen at 16.

- Labellists: More of a 15–25 lad thing. These guys love big name labels and like nothing better than a night out at a superclub with their mates. Aspire to the 'Posh and Becks lifestyle'.
- Regulars: Laid-back and straightforward, these guys and girls, aged 16 upwards, are the Gap generation, a group that knows what it likes and likes to know where it is going. Stability and belonging are important values.

As with any segmentation model we could have subtly nuanced a further ten clusters had we prioritised absolute precision over a model the business could recognise, appreciate and work with. We stuck to six and quickly invested our energy in defining their exact profile in full technicolour detail for each of the key markets in Western Europe, such that the organisation was crystal clear who the different groups were. In sizing the clusters to determine their exact significance and provide some harder quantitative edge to our profiling of them, we worked with RISC based in Paris, inserting a series of brand, clothing and shopping-specific questions to their annual lifestyle study.

In order for the analysis process to work, we spent two days with the RISC team in the field, looking at products, brands, and consumers, visiting both bars and clothing stores. As a result of that, we had a common approach and language which helped enormously in the work. Coming out of the process, we had a much deeper understanding of the segments – and we had one additional segment, which we, in our clothing-focused world, hadn't thought about: the 'Out of Fashion' – young people for whom fashion matters very little. Think Saffy in *AbFab*.

Quantification in number of people (million)

TYPES IN EUR		EUR 5 COUNTRIES 15/35 Y.O = 37% TOTAL = 108 965 000
The Cultural Creatives	5	5 448 250
The Modernists	6	6 537 900
The Sensible Choosers	13	14 165 450
The Edge	11	11 986 150
The Fast Fashion Flirts	11	11 986 150
The Labelists	12	13 075 800
The Regulars	27	29 420 550
The Out of Fashion	16	17 434 400

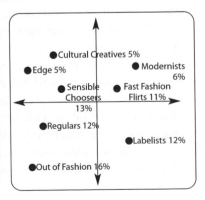

Figure A2.3 Customer clusters

The model defined and agreed, the focus quickly shifted to applying this understanding to addressing the key brand and market questions.

Brand positioning

Having rather lost its way in the early 1980s, the company had effectively been rescued by a strategy that focused the entire business on the ultimate unique truth about the brand: the 501® jeans. Throughout the subsequent years of success, the business had thought it knew what made the brand unique. It was the Original denim jeans brand, the inventor of the five-pocket Western jean, the brand that made all other denim jeans brands feel like pale imitations. From this was born the now legendary Original Jeans campaign. A consumer in Italy once put it very elegantly: 'When I pull on any other jeans I am just pulling on a pair of jeans. When I pull on my 501's, I can hear the Harley in my ears.'

This absolute focus on owning originality was and remains right. Problems arose, however, when the brand's expression of originality (in product, retail and communication) started to become overly formulaic and frankly dull. The brand had lost sight of what had originally excited the consumer about its claim to be 'the Original' back in 1985, and had become preoccupied with preserving its aura of originality. And that aura in the consumers' eyes became a rather tedious obsession with tradition and denim historiography.

From an organisational point of view, the dynamic was very easy to understand. The 501® jeans product and the Original Jeans campaign had effectively saved the business and turned it into a hugely profitable 'machine'. Any attempt to move away from a proven formula was met with mistrust. Originality switched from being the motivating anchor point for the brand to being a straitjacket on any form of brand innovation. The new retail format for the Original Levi's® Stores rolled out in 1996 was temples to the brand's past history. The design concept itself was called 'a General Store'. Buy a pair of 501® jeans from one of these stores and you would be rewarded with a brown paper bag branded with the marque of the two horse logo and designed to transport your groceries 'down the sidewalk'. Tune into MTV in spring or fall around the time of the proven media calendar, and you would find 60 seconds of what was usually rather witty sexual nostalgia for a time when the garment of choice for young Americans with an attitude was a pair of 501® jeans: a formula whose original power ultimately started to wane when the consumer saw it for what it was and Levi's® acknowledged as much in its own Clayman execution.

The brand vision team reflected on all of this, and concluded that the brand had no option but to reassert its original point of distinction, but in a much more relevant way. Levi's® meant blue jeans. Blue jeans had finally gone off trend, the brand had been powerless to stop that and had fallen with the market. There was no point in running away from the problem. There was no place to run to. The inventor of the blue jean had to make blue jeans cool again.

Implicit in this positioning strategy was the recognition that originality could never again be mistaken just for tradition and authenticity. What connected young people to the brand's originality in the late 1980s was the combination of the brand's claim to be the one true original and the rebellious sexually charged payload of the young pioneers who shaped America back in the 1850s, 1950s, 1960s and 1970s and wore jeans to prove it. The young Berliner who stood on the Berlin wall as it came down with a banner which read, 'You can have Marx or you can have Levi's®', epitomised the brand's true distinction.

Levi's® is, was and should always be the definitive source of denim jeanswear. It invented the blue jean, and its role should be to keep it perpetually fresh, interesting and true unto itself. The umbrella brand vision, the scary goal that serves as an inspirational rallying call across all organisational activity, is the intention 'to equip young people to change their world'.

Consumer driven brand innovation

So the map of the terrain was defined and the route decided. The journey could now begin. We talked earlier about an introspective business with a highly developed sense of innophobia and an aversion to consumer information. The first step in the journey was to build a process that would ensure the business would never again be able to let the consumer quite so far out of its sight.

The Youth Panel

The key tool that was developed by the Levi Strauss & Co Research Team and Added Value came to be known unceremoniously as the Youth Panel. Initially, it was used as a source of illumination; over time it became a powerful litmus test of innovation as it was developing.

It is essentially a regularly refreshed, extremely select, qualitative consumer panel focused on the consumer typologies we believe exercise greatest influence on the dynamics of change within the casual apparel market, the Modernist and the Edge consumers. The panel has been built up in each of the most fashion significant European cities (Berlin, Milan, Paris, Barcelona and London) and comprises between 50 and 100 of the most fashion-forward youth you could hope to meet. We hand select them individually from the art/media/photographic schools of each city by stationing our most target friendly moderators in the bars, clubs, shops and other places they frequent. It is time-consuming and expensive, but it has revolutionised the quality and the credibility of the insight we are able to gather. To complement the trendsetting consumers, and to ensure that we are equally exposed to the consumers from whom the majority of our sales will flow, the panel also covers both Regular Guys and Regular Girls, often more surprising to the design team than the more fashion-involved respondents.

The panel is convened twice a year to fit into the line development calendar ahead of the spring and fall line briefs (when the first sketches are laid out). Meetings take place in environments selected to be sympathetic to the target rather than airport or audio convenient. In London we use a collection of artists' studios above a tube station in Clerkenwell.

In the past the contribution research could make to the innovation process was dismissed for the usual rearview mirror reasons. Designers wouldn't waste time listening to mainstream consumers because they knew they had to aim ahead of the curve, and there was no one to talk to whose view on where the curve was going they would respect. The panel members, the environments we use, and the vocal support of the most senior management in the business have changed all that. We now get up to 15 people drawn from the brand and design teams attending each of the panel sessions and using the information.

We experimented with a few different techniques to ensure panel learning was professionally interpreted and appropriately communicated. As with any other business, the insight we gather is only as good as its application. And it only gets applied right when it is properly absorbed. We attached great significance to finding the right media to convey the message to best effect. Fancy multimedia CD ROMs didn't crack it. They became occasional reference documents when what we needed was a living tool. The inspiration came by thinking about the internal audience as any media planner would its external audience. When were we most likely to find a slice of their attention? Easy really – on planes, trains and sofas. The bibles of the fashion industry are style magazines, so we needed to package our knowledge as a style magazine. *YP* was born and is now into its sixth edition, with an internal print run of over 500. It's a simple tool but it means everybody who needs to be close to the consumer in the business has an accessible bag-sized reminder of where the market is moving and what the key challenges are for the brand.

Product innovation

The brand vision team had laid down a clear challenge. The business needed to reassert the brand's leadership in denim by revolutionising the product, its

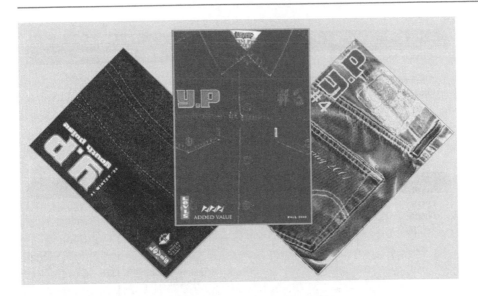

Figure A2.4 *YP:* sharing insights from the Youth Panel

retail presentation and its mode of communication with the target. Product had to be the first priority, for it was clearly the most fundamental problem plaguing the brand. Levi's® had created the first denim blueprint back in 1853. It now needed to make a similar creative leap. Two pieces of work were initiated in parallel. A crack team of young designers and marketers were locked up for two weeks and given the task of coming up with the next denim blueprint.

Meanwhile, the research team assembled the first panel sessions in London and Paris with the specific goal of recapturing the magic that denim had lost. Panel members included students of photography, web design, fabric technology and fashion. While they confirmed the by now evident decline of denim – even the *Daily Mail* had picked up on the story by this stage – they helped explain the fundamental problem with the jeans product was: 'It's not that we are down on denim, it's just that no one has done anything interesting with denim for so long that we are bored; more bored than you could possibly imagine.'

In tabling the problem so simply, they opened our eyes to a number of dimensions of the core jean concept which could be experimented with: the core characteristics of the fabric itself, the core characteristics of the five-pocket Western jean, the notion of blending denim with other fabrics, and the utilisation of denim in creating entirely new non-pant products.

While some of these ideas fell into the realms of the fantastical, two insights in particular had particular resonance with the work the design team were doing. The panel were very clear that jeans had traded for some time on

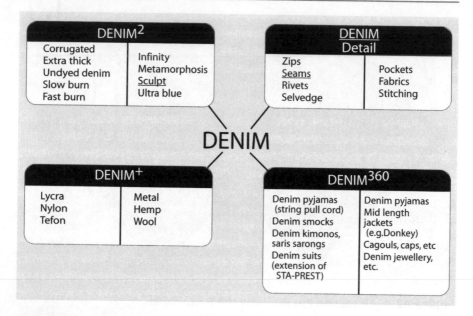

Figure A2.5 Expanding dimensions of the jeans concept

being the most comfortable garment known to humanity, the famous 'second skin', and yet when looked at from a pure comfort perspective, a five-pocket Western jean was far from perfect (and meanwhile new fabrics and cuts in utility clothing had made big strides in this area).

Second, the most unique quality of the fabric itself was perceived to be the extraordinary sculpt and drape of denim, most obvious immediately after washing or when drying, but evident also in use. Every jean assumes unique folds and drapes in accordance with the garment and its owner.

> *No other fabric does that and it could be so easily exploited at the design stage. It's like they are trying to hold the fabric back from doing what it was originally intended to do. If you played with the seams, you could do a lot with the drape ...*

All innovation processes are a mixture of logic, imagination and serendipity. Here, the design team found strong spontaneous confirmation from a panel they respected that the direction they were most interested in pursuing had a real consumer rationale and some real market potential. That was February. By May prototype products of Red and Levi's® Engineered Jeans™ were available for testing, and by early December the first modified examples of Red were on sale in select distribution in London and Paris. A full scale launch of Levi's® Engineered Jeans™ followed in February 2002.

Figure A2.6 The sculpt and drape of denim

Other applications of the Youth Panel

Like all good tools, the panel has come to serve a number of useful functions, not all of which were envisaged from the outset. It provides perhaps the best indication the business has of how much momentum a particular trend has (left) in it, and therefore serves to guide both general business forecasting and specific product lifecycle management. It provides a continuous input into the company's sponsorship activity, and plays an important troubleshooting role. Every second quarter the brand and design teams dedicate a day to working with the insights coming out of the panel. It helps set the strategic agenda, and also enables some very effective and immediate troubleshooting. Products in line development have been dropped entirely based on panel feedback

Figure A2.7 Levi's Engineered Jeans™

(previously unthinkable), and rapid response retail teams have been flown into Berlin the day after one of these events to address issues that were arising around the opening of the new opinion-leading gallery store concept in Berlin.

Retail innovation

From the outset it had been apparent that the brand needed strikingly new product, but that if we failed to rejuvenate the retail presentation of that product, it would die at the moment of truth. Having re-established the brand vision and reinvented the product offer at the core of the Levi's® brand, we were therefore faced with the challenge of ensuring that the right (targeted) consumer meets the right product at point of sale. Based on the basic premise that innovation only helps to drive brand equity and sales when visible and understandable to consumers, we worked with Added Value to find a way to first segment our distribution, and secondly reinvent the way the Levi's® brand is displayed at point of sale.

To ensure that the right product meets the right consumer, the segmentation had to be consumer inspired. To achieve this, we conducted a series of consumer workshops and accompanied shops which helped us identify the various consumer shopping modes, from the most specific 'replacement shopping', when a product has worn out and you need to buy a new one, and preferably the exact same item (a lot of regular guys should be able to nod to that one) to the most unfocused 'networking' where talking to, and being seen with, the right people in a place which just happens also to sell clothes. Because different types of consumers have a tendency to shop in different ways, the workshops were based on the typologies that we had developed earlier in the year.

Now, consumers can't tell you what retail 'segment' they shop in, but they can tell you which stores they go to and what they do when they get there. From that information we conducted a visual audit which allowed us to construct a series of visual cues through which we could identify specific segments.

The segmentation basically covers three layers: Leading Edge Originators where both fashion and street trends start, but which are unlikely to be commercially huge, Trend Diffusers where the latest fashion becomes slightly more commercial but where only the most daring regular consumers shop, and finally a mainstream tier divided into retail professional and traditional retailers. Within each tier, we identified specific segments depending on the look and feel of the store and product range.

The power of having established a total picture of our current distribution was that we could identify where a product like Engineered Jeans™ had to be present in order to come face to face with the consumer who was most likely to adopt it. Because we understood the predominant shopping modes in the stores, we were now able to adapt our display for different segments.

With this in place, we then internally developed training programmes, in order to help store staff recognise the different shopping modes in order to best serve their needs in the store. It means that they can help the guy who wants to 'replacement shop' get his pair of jeans quickly and then get out of the store, while they know to leave the girl who wants to browse and allow her time to explore on her own.

The work had thrown up one fundamental and large problem. The European network of franchised Original Levi's® Stores, and major corners in multibrand stores, which were supposed to be the most adept at demonstrating the Levi's® brand at retail, all suffered from being essentially about replacement shopping, and extremely weak on encouraging browsing and discovery. At a time when we were aimed at enticing consumers to discover that there is more to the Levi's® brand than your dad's 501® jeans, the lack of browsing and discovery presented a major barrier. It screamed out for innovation in the way we sold jeans.

Looking at the Original Levi's® Stores and major shop-in-shops, the design response to the challenge that the initial work had helped highlight took its inspiration from fresh fruit and fish! Unlike jeans which are hidden away in stacks, difficult to see, hard to touch, the design agency hypothesised that fresh fruit and fish was a perfect example of a display which would tempt the eye and inspire the consumer to buy.

As a result the stores were transformed, moving away from the traditional denim wall, to a flexible wall system which provided a canvas upon which we could lay products flat in lasagne style or hang them over pegs in spaghetti style. Either way, it allowed consumers to see, touch and discover the product range. With this practical shift came a series of changes within the visual merchandising techniques – posters and product explanations – which helped bring the brand and the product range to life. The result has been staggering; both in terms of sell out and in terms of brand image generated.

The power of the initial consumer-inspired segmentation work rallied the company around a common understanding of distribution points, allowing us to ensure that the right consumer meets the right product at point of sale. This has played a huge part in laying out the challenge for the reinvention of the Levi's® brand retail environment. To avoid going stale at point of sale again, we have established an annual process of review and design evolution which starts and ends with consumer feedback.

SO DID WE REALLY MAKE A DIFFERENCE?

If you believed the business pages you could be forgiven for thinking that the turnaround at Levi Strauss & Co hasn't really happened yet. There are two answers to the question. First, where the brand vision programme has been implemented, principally in Europe, a business which was in free fall has succeeded in reversing the decline. Second, when a business declines as rapidly as Levi Strauss & Co did, recovery does not come in one season. The original strategy came in three stages: regain control, stabilise and grow. Revenue is now back under control, and the business has a very stable base from which we are seeing good signs of equity improvement after four years of continuous decline, and the first green shoots of growth. LEJ has sold four million units since launch, thereby surpassing the performance of most of the collection of emergent competitors at whose hands we had suffered in 1998 and 1999.

Success always has many parents, and there was no shortage of contributors to this story. If you were to ask what really made the difference, then there are three drivers without which it could not have happened. The first is undoubtedly that the business had a burning platform, the like of which has rarely been seen. The company had no option but to act. The second is charismatic leadership. Robert Hansen was appointed Brand President in September 1999 and drove the implementation of the brand vision with extraordinary energy and focus. His task is now to repeat the achievement in the United States.

Third, and equally important, is that the culture of the business and the people within it was transformed. People who had never been given space to grow, developed capabilities that only 12 months previously would have seemed unimaginable. People who had the capabilities but no space to exercise them found that at last they could.

And what role did research play in this? We raised the alarm and didn't stop shouting until the business could no longer ignore the facts that were staring it square in the face. This bought us the credibility to partner in building a genuinely consumer driven business. Because we got on our soap box and managed to inspire action from the organisation, the company in Europe was able to begin preparing for the turnaround, while elsewhere the company was still unconvinced that we were in decline. By being crystal clear and compelling about the need to drive major product and retail innovation, we helped shape the agenda for the reinvention of the Levi's® brand.

None of what we have done from a technical research point of view is brain surgery. We didn't waste time developing fancy research models to explain what was going on. Instead we focused our energy on understanding consumers and making sure that the organisation did. In so doing, we managed to shape the agenda and build a role for research in running the company.

Research is now a totally integrated function in the business whose goal, on both strategic and tactical projects is to inspire the organisation to act – a state of play unthinkable four years ago.

The Brand Bullseye and the story of Pilsner Urquell

As pointed out in the body of the book, there are many ways of capturing a brand positioning. This is the Bullseye methodology, and to illustrate it I have used the real case study of Pilsner Urquell.

South African Breweries (now SABMiller) bought the Pilsner Urquell brand in 1999 with the objective of reviving it as one of the top international brands. I say 'revive', because Pilsner Urquell was one of the first truly international beers. At the turn of the last century a train left Pilzen in the Czech republic, as the country is now called, every day carrying this unique beer to top capitals around the world. Under the communist regime the brand and the company stagnated but the beer remained as wonderful as ever. Pilsner refers to its appellation of Pilzen – only a pilsner from Pilzen is a true pilsner beer – and Urquell means 'original source'. Pilsner Urquell is still made using a unique process that gives it quite simply more of what a beer should be. It is very bitter but also has high residual sugars, giving it a bitter sweet taste that is delicious, refreshing and moreish. The visionary brewmaster, originally from Bavaria, was a true pioneer and Pilsner Urquell was the first clear golden beer. Up until 1842 when he created the product and the brand, all beers were dark or cloudy. I could go on, and on, and on. The fact is that this brand has more heritage and mythology than you could ever dream of, and it was a dream positioning exercise.

There are two types of positioning project. In the first you are creating a positioning for a brand, in other words trying to conjure up the motivating differentiators that will give the brand an edge, a reason to buy. In the second you are effectively cutting a raw diamond: there is a real sparkling heart to the brand and you have to cut or hone the facets of the brand that present it in its best light. I had worked on Guinness which was like this, but to be honest many others before had shaped the diamond (one of the experts working on Guinness had even come up with the diamond analogy) and we were really just polishing. But with Pilsner Urquell we had the true gem – an outstanding product, with more to say than you could find space for and virgin territory.

The brand had been presented – 'It's the original and best pilsner' – but never positioned.

The exercise took six months and it is interesting to see the material that was developed to identify the range of positioning territories. There were actually 'steelomatics' produced (videos where you use material taken from movies and other commercials, cleverly edited to bring a positioning idea alive) and used in the exploratory research as well as highly finished concept boards which are shown on the following pages (Figures A3.1–3.3).

The route with the most potential was 'Drink different'. It tapped into something that really resonated with our target audience, the attraction of a true original. Jeremy Bullmore has explained the attraction of fame that lies at the heart of great brands. We like to meet famous people just as we like to buy famous brands. But what would you give to meet Nelson Mandela, or John Lennon, or Eric Cantona? These people were originals, one-offs who redefined the way we think about statesmen, musicians and footballers. Their presence is not just appealing, it is inspirational. (See Figures A3.4–3.6.)

There were many long discussions and the odd cul de sac in how the positioning was developed and refined, but here is the final version, expressed in the Bullseye format. It was a great brand to work on and a great project, one that has delivered something that should inspire great marketing. It certainly inspired one of the best pieces of packaging redesign in the category masterminded by the best designer I have ever worked with, Dave Brown of Enterprise IG. (See Figure A3.7.)

While handing out the credits I need also to acknowledge that Ben Wood of Added Value was the driving force behind the development of the positioning, and Mark Luce and Phil Plowman were supportive and inspiring clients.

The reader might be interested to know who now has the responsibility of ensuring this brand achieves its international potential (Tony van Kralingen and Ian Penhale, CEO and Marketing Director respectively of SABMiller Czech Republic, having already driven Pilsner Urquell to even higher shares in its domestic market). Let me sign off:

Mark Sherrington
Group Marketing Director
SABMiller Plc

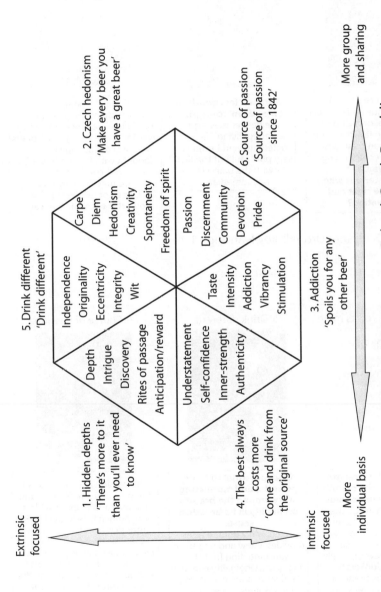

Figure A3.1 Range of assessed positionings

1. Hidden depths

Helps reinforce/build the brand's mystique and projects an aspirational drinker profile but lacks real relevance (more special occasion, wind down, connoisseur, challenging product).
Why be mysterious when you can be clear and motivating?

2. Czech hedonism

Another 'feel good/ carpe diem' concept.
The deeper message about living life differently and better is very powerful but the link with the brand is not immediate.

3. Addiction

Original language to capture/dramatise the unique drinking experience yet strong aversion to knocking other beers and rejected as hype by many (poor fit with PU's understated self-confidence).
Too functional overall:
Does not ladder up to a powerful extrinsic message.

Figure A3.2 Pilsner Urquell: key learnings 1

4. The best... costs more

Reinforced the strength and appeal of the brand's intrinsics and underlined the need to leverage them fully. Motivating inherent message about the drinker (discerning, mature, man of integrity) However, unlikely to prompt drinkers to reappraise the brand or significantly increase its relevance.

5. Drink different

Clear potential to build powerful and motivating story around the brand's originality in its broadest sense.
The original golden beer provides a new and engaging substantiation for PU's originality. Originality can also ladder up to an aspirational and inspirational extrinsic message.

6. Source of passion

The passion and devotion of the brewers is motivating and credible and helps provide a more human face to the brand's intrinsics. The claim however that this beer (or any beer) inspires such passion in drinkers lacks credibility for most.
Passion needs to work as the take-out rather than the stimulus.

Figure A3.3 Pilsner Urquell: key learnings 2

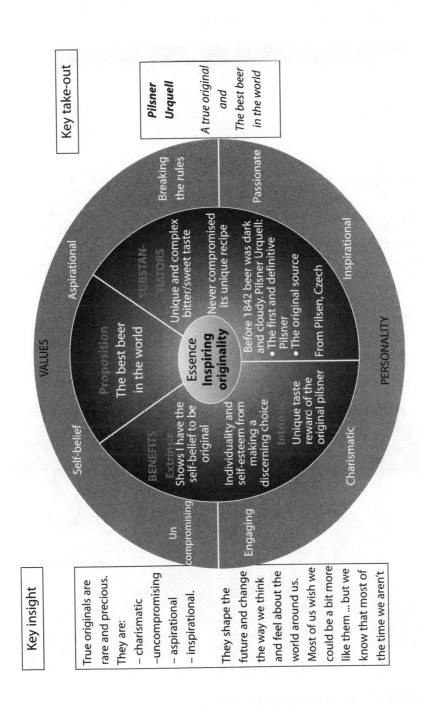

Key take-out

Pilsner Urquell

A true original and The best beer in the world

Key insight

True originals are rare and precious. They are:

– charismatic
–uncompromising
– aspirational
– inspirational.

They shape the future and change the way we think and feel about the world around us. Most of us wish we could be a bit more like them ... but we know that most of the time we aren't

VALUES

Aspirational

Self-belief

Breaking the rules

Un compromising

Proposition
The best beer in the world

SUBSTAN-TIATORS

Unique and complex bitter/sweet taste

Never compromised its unique recipe

Essence
Inspiring originality

Before 1842 beer was dark and cloudy. Pilsner Urquell:
• The first and definitive Pilsner
• The original source

From Pilsen, Czech

BENEFITS

Extrinsic
Shows I have the self-belief to be original

Individuality and self-esteem from making a discerning choice

Intrinsic
Unique taste reward of the original pilsner

Engaging

Charismatic

Inspirational

Passionate

PERSONALITY

Figure A3.4 Pilsner Urquell: brand positioning

- There are many different types of originality. We need a tight definition of Pilsner Urquell's originality.

IS	ISN'T
• Different for a reason	• Different for the sake of it
• A leap of faith	• A shot in the dark
• Extraordinary	• Wacky, quirky
• Gifted	• Intellectual
• Innate	• Put on
• Generous	• Selfish

Pilsner Urquell rewrote the rules for a reason: to create an exceptional and definitive style of beer and bring joy to generations of beer drinkers the world over. Pilsner Urquell started the Golden Age of beer drinking and made people reappraise the whole category.

Figure A3.5 Tight definitions: how do we define originality?

Figure A3.6 Pilsner Urquell: brand calling card

Old   New

Figure A3.7 Pilsner Urquell: the old and new designs

Notes

1 Hammel, Gary and Prahalad, C. K. (1996) *Competing for the Future*, Cambridge, MA: Harvard Business School Press.
2 Collins, James C. and Porras, Jerry I. (2002) *Built to Last: Successful Habits of Visionary Companies*, London: Harper Business Essentials.
3 Bullmore, Jeremy (2003) 'Posh Spice and Persil', *Behind the Scenes in Advertising, 3rd* edn, World Advertising Research Center.
4. Pichot, Gifford III (1985) *Intrapreneuring: Why You Don't Have to Leave the Corporation to Become an Entrepreneur*, New York: Harper & Row.
5. Bower, Joseph L. and Christensen, Clayton M. (1995) 'Disruptive technologies, catching the wave', *Harvard Business Review* (January), pp. 43–53.
6. Bogle, N. (Nov. 2001), 'Brand Fame – the new currency?', *Market Leader*, 16, pp. 47–52.
7. Morgan, A. (1999) *Eating the Big Fish*, Chichester: John Wiley.